PUBLISHER'S NOTE

V&S Publishers has carved a significant niche in the publishing industry over the last decade, having successfully published more than 1000 titles across 9 languages spanning over 50 subject categories. Being known for the quality of content, we have built a reputation of excellence and reliability. We have consistently delivered **"Value & Substance"** to our readers, through a wide range of titles across a variety of genres covering school books, fiction and non-fiction that caters to different people from every section of the society.

The **Olympiad Guidebooks for classes 1-10** across all subjects, launched almost a decade ago, under the **GEN X Imprint**, became a go-to-source for the school students in no time, owing to their invaluable and substantive content written in a guidebook pattern,.

Having successfully sold a million copies of the same and in response to demand by both students as well as shopkeepers nationwide; we now present before you our newly launched **Olympiad Workbook Series**, designed for **classes 1-10 across 4 subjects**.

The workbooks are meticulously curated by a team of experienced educators, researchers and subject matter experts, edited by professionals and peer reviewed by teachers. The team has poured its efforts and expertise into creating a crisp and concise workbook which will help and guide the students to the path of success in Olympiad exams. The **MCQs** identified will not only help in scoring top marks in Olympiads but also inculcate a sense of deeper understanding of the subject, by way of solving **HOTS** and referring to complete solutions at the end of the book.

Here we present our new release– **OLYMPIAD WORKBOOK (IMO) CLASS–3** having following features:

- ☞ Based on the latest syllabi
- ☞ MCQs with comprehensive coverage of topics
- ☞ HOTS Questions liberally included
- ☞ A dedicated chapter on logical reasoning
- ☞ Model test paper for thorough practice
- ☞ Sample OMR sheet for real time simulation

We have made sure through our best efforts, that this workbook strictly follows the latest syllabi and patterns of the Olympiad Examination.

As **V&S Publishers** continuously strive to enhance the readability and maintain the credibility of our academic publications, we seek the support of our valuable readers in influencing and enriching the lives of future generations of students.

P.S. While every care has been taken to ensure the correctness of the content, if you come across any error, howsoever minor, do not hesitate to discuss with teachers while pointing that out to us in no uncertain terms.

We wish you all the best for your exams!

DISTINCTIVE FEATURES

01 Learning Objectives

They list the whole chapter as subtopics, helping the teachers to guide children in a step-by-step manner.

02 Multiple Choice Questions

MCQs act as an excellent learning aid, helping you to understand and work on your mistakes.

03 HOTS (Achievers Section)

The High Order Thinking Questions aim to help the student to solve Application-based questions and gain practical understanding of the subject.

04 Model Test Paper

Model test paper are provided at the end of each book, which help the student to test the knowledge which they have gained after thorough reading of all chapters.

05 Answer Key

Detailed Answer Key along with explanations aid the pupil to indentify, understand the mistakes they make during the course of Olympiad preparation.

OLYMPIAD WORKBOOK

INTERNATIONAL MATHEMATICS OLYMPIAD

- **01** Learning Objectives
- **02** Multiple Choice Questions
- **03** HOTS (Achievers Section)
- **04** Model Test Paper
- **05** Answer Keys and Solutions
- **06** OMR Answer Sheet

V&S PUBLISHERS

Published by:

V&S PUBLISHERS

F-2/16, Ansari road, Daryaganj, New Delhi-110002
☎ 23240026, 23240027 • *Fax:* 011-23240028
✉ info@vspublishers.com • 🌐 www.vspublishers.com

 **Online Brandstore: amazon.in/vspublishers**

Regional Office : Hyderabad
5-1-707/1, Brij Bhawan (Beside Central Bank of India Lane)
Bank Street, Koti, Hyderabad - 500 095
☎ 040-24737290
✉ vspublishershyd@gmail.com

Follow us on:   

BUY OUR BOOKS FROM: | AMAZON | | FLIPKART |

DISCLAIMER

While every attempt has been made to provide accurate and timely information in this book, neither the author nor the publisher assumes any responsibility for errors, unintended omissions or commissions detected therein. The author and publisher makes no representation or warranty with respect to the comprehensiveness or completeness of the contents provided.

All matters included have been simplified under professional guidance for general information only, without any warranty for applicability on an individual. Any mention of an organization or a website in the book, by way of citation or as a source of additional information, doesn't imply the endorsement of the content either by the author or the publisher. It is possible that websites cited may have changed or removed between the time of editing and publishing the book.

Results from using the expert opinion in this book will be totally dependent on individual circumstances and factors beyond the control of the author and the publisher.

It makes sense to elicit advice from well informed sources before implementing the ideas given in the book. The reader assumes full responsibility for the consequences arising out from reading this book.

For proper guidance, it is advisable to read the book under the watchful eyes of parents/guardian. The buyer of this book assumes all responsibility for the use of given materials and information.

The copyright of the entire content of this book rests with the author/publisher. Any infringement/transmission of the cover design, text or illustrations, in any form, by any means, by any entity will invite legal action and be responsible for consequences thereon.

CONTENTS

NUMBER SYSTEM

LEARNING OBJECTIVES

➤ Numerals and Number Sense (4-Digit Numbers)
➤ Face Value and Place Value
➤ Expanded Form and Number Name
➤ Ascending and Descending Order

MULTIPLE CHOICE QUESTIONS

1. Which one of the following is an even number?
   (A) 733
   (B) 550
   (C) 241
   (D) 89

2. Match the columns.

Column I	Column II
(1) 7000 + 400 + 20 + 6	(i) 7067
(2) 7000 + 400 + 0 + 6 + 0	(ii) 766
(3) 700 + 60 + 6	(iii) 7406
(4) 7000 + 0 + 60 + 6 + 7	(iv) 7426

   (A) 1 – i, 2 – ii, 3 – iii, 4 – iv
   (B) 1 – ii, 2 – iii, 3 – i, 4 – iv
   (C) 1 – iv, 2 – iii, 3 – ii, – 4 i
   (D) 1 – ii, 2 – iv, 3 – iii, 4 – i

3. The largest 3-digit number is __________.
   (A) 999   (B) 899
   (C) 889   (D) 988

4. Find the odd one out.
   14, 2, 12, 5, 10
   (A) 2   (B) 5
   (C) 10   (D) 14

5. The largest 3-digit number which is even is __________.
   (A) 998   (B) 102
   (C) 888   (D) 999

6. The sum of numbers from 1 to 12 is ____.
   (A) 78   (B) 59
   (C) 73   (D) 71

7. What is the face value of the underlined digit in the number given below:

   38$\underline{4}$55

   (A) 4   (B) 5
   (C) 3   (D) 8

8. What is the expanded form of given number 12,554?
   (A) 12 + 5 + 5 + 4
   (B) 12,000 + 500 + 50 + 4
   (C) 1200 + 54 + 5
   (D) 1200 + 50 + 45

9. Find the greatest 3-digit number from the following:
   341, 199, 111, 627, 245
   (A) 341   (B) 627
   (C) 199   (D) 245

10. Find the smallest 3-digit number from the following:

341, 199, 111, 627, 245

(A) 627   (B) 111

(C) 245   (D) 199

11. Choose the correct option.

(A) 371 > 231   (B) 591 < 326

(C) 140 > 200   (D) 529 = 226

Direction (12-13): Consider the following numbers to answer the questions:

4   17   9   45   22   19   12   34

12. If numbers are to be selected from the above list such that odd numbers are to be picked in ascending order, then what would be the sequence of numbers?

(A) 4, 12, 22, 34   (B) 9, 17, 19, 45

(C) 34, 22, 12, 4   (D) 45, 19, 17, 9

13. If numbers are to be selected from the above list such that even numbers are to be picked in descending order, then what would be the sequence of numbers?

(A) 4, 12, 22, 34

(B) 9, 17, 19, 45

(C) 34, 22, 12, 4

(D) 45, 19, 17, 9

14. The smallest 4-digit number formed by the digits 5, 6, 0, 7 is ___________.

(A) 0567   (B) 5067

(C) 6057   (D) 5076

15. What is the successor of largest 3-digit number?

(A) 998   (B) 1000

(C) 999   (D) None of these

16. Rahul has 961 coins with him. Write 961 in words.

(A) Seven hundred ninety-six

(B) Seven hundred sixty-nine

(C) Nine hundred seventy-one

(D) Nine hundred sixty-one

17. The following table shows the money each child have.

Children	Money (₹)
Naina	20 hundreds
Tanu	3 hundreds 5 ones
Sona	56 tens
Shiv	9 hundreds

Which of the following statements is incorrect?

(A) Naina has maximum money.

(B) Sona has minimum money.

(C) Shiv has ₹900.

(D) Sona has ₹560.

18. Rohan has following cards:

4	9	7	6

Which is the least possible 4-digit number that Rohan can form by using above cards?

(A) 4679

(B) 9647

(C) 4697

(D) 4967

19. Tanya has a book that contains 4579 pages. Sapna has a book that contains 4673 pages. Kapil has a book that contains 7463 pages. Whose book has maximum number of pages?

(A) Tanya

(B) Sapna

(C) Kapil

(D) Both Sapna and Kapil

20. Jyoti has ₹9 thousands 2 hundreds 61 ones. Write this in numeral form.

(A) ₹9261

(B) ₹92610

(C) ₹926

(D) ₹2619

21. Which of these has the smallest value?
    (A) 1/2 of 160
    (B) Half of 180
    (C) 12 × 13
    (D) 2 times of (5 × 5)

22. How many two-digit numbers between 10 to 40 have the digits at ten's place smaller than that of one's place?
    (A) 19   (B) 20
    (C) 21   (D) 22

23. Which of the following has same value as 2618?
    (A) 200 + 618
    (B) 2000 + 600 + 18
    (C) 2000 + 68
    (D) 2008 + 17

24. Which of the following set of numbers is in the order from the lowest to the highest?
    (A) 982, 985, 989, 789, 925, 1025
    (B) 1920, 1902, 9102, 2109, 9201
    (C) 9876, 9768, 9678, 8976, 8796, 6879
    (D) 1920, 9102, 9321, 9468, 9768

25. Which of the given abacus shows the number less than 1345?

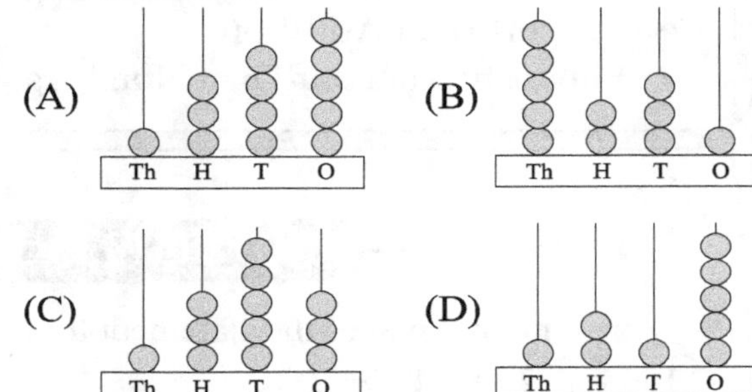

Darken Your Choice with HB Pencil

1.	A B C D	6.	A B C D	11.	A B C D	16.	A B C D	21.	A B C D
2.	A B C D	7.	A B C D	12.	A B C D	17.	A B C D	22.	A B C D
3.	A B C D	8.	A B C D	13.	A B C D	18.	A B C D	23.	A B C D
4.	A B C D	9.	A B C D	14.	A B C D	19.	A B C D	24.	A B C D
5.	A B C D	10.	A B C D	15.	A B C D	20.	A B C D	25.	A B C D

COMPUTATION OPERATIONS 

LEARNING OBJECTIVES

➤ Addition of Four-Digit Numbers
➤ Properties of Addition
➤ Subtraction of Four-Digit Numbers
➤ Multiplication of 4-Digit Numbers
➤ Opposite of Multiplication
➤ Division of 4-Digit Numbers

MULTIPLE CHOICE QUESTIONS

1. Which number makes the statement true?

   $1508 + 125 = 2407 + ?$

   (A) 226
   (B) 774
   (C) 126
   (D) − 774

2. Which options complete the pattern?

   $4 + 5 = $ _____________

   $40 + 50 = $ _____________

   $400 + 500 = $ _____________

   (A) 9, 90, 900
   (B) 9, 99,990
   (C) 9,90, 990
   (D) 9, 99, 900

3. Which numbers complete the pattern?

   _____________ $+ 6 = 9$

   _____________ $+ 60 = 90$

   _____________ $+ 600 = 900$

   (A) 2, 22, 200
   (B) 2, 20, 220
   (C) 2, 22, 220
   (D) 3, 30, 300

4. Look at the table below. What is rule for the table?

Input	Output
623	636
544	557
388	401
279	292

   (A) Add 22
   (B) Add 23
   (C) Add 13
   (D) Add 12

5. State whether the following statements are true or false.

   i. $5746 + 2222$ is as same as $3984 + 3984$.
   ii. If we add 777 to 7777 we will get 8554.
   iii. If we add 89 to 6789 we will get 6879.
   iv. $3000 + 175$ is more than $2981 + 179$.

   (A) TTFT
   (B) FFTT
   (C) TFTF
   (D) FTFT

6. Which number makes the statement true?

   $66 - ? = 80 - 32$

   (A) 68
   (B) 48
   (C) 58
   (D) 18

7. Which number complete the pattern?

$6 - 5 =$ _______

$60 - 50 =$ _______

$600 - 500 =$ _______

$6000 - 5000 =$ _______

(A) 1, 11, 111, 1111

(B) 1, 10, 100, 1000

(C) 11, 110, 111

(D) 10, 110, 111

8. Which number complete the pattern?

$9 - 5 =$ _______

$90 - 50 =$ _______

$900 - 500 =$ _______

(A) 4, 40, 400   (B) 5, 500, 550

(C) 5, 50, 500   (D) 5, 55, 550

9. Look at the table below. What is rule for the table?

Input	Output
345	331
456	442
789	775
910	896

(A) Subtract 10   (B) Subtract 14

(C) Subtract 16   (D) Subtract 25

10. Look at the table. What is the rule for the table?

Input	Output
300	330
200	230
100	130
400	430

(A) Add 30   (B) Add 15

(C) Add 20   (D) Add 25

11. The product of '0' and any number is __________.

(A) 1   (B) 0

(C) Both of them   (D) None of these

12. Choose the correct option.

$10 \times$ _______ $= 90$

(A) 8   (B) 9

(C) 19   (D) 90

13. Choose the correct option.

__________ $\times 9 = 36$

(A) 4   (B) 2

(C) 8   (D) 7

14. Which one of the following statement is incorrect?

Statement A: 12 pairs of socks are 24 socks.

Statement B: 5 rainbows have 35 colors.

Statement C: 8 dice have 45 faces.

Statement D: 4 Tic-tac-toe games have 36 boxes.

(A) C   (B) D

(C) A   (D) B

15. $(4757 \times 403) \times 2 =$ _______

(A) $(4757 \times 403) + 2$

(B) $(4757 \times 2) + 403$

(C) $4757 \times (403 \times 2)$

(D) None of these

16. $4 + 4 + 4 + 4 + 4 + 4 + 4 = 28$

There are 7 groups of number 4. Which is the correct way to write this?

(A) 4×28 (B) $28 \div 4$

(C) 7×4 (D) 4×8

17. Which two pairs are same?

(A) $3 \div 3$, $16 \div 2$ (B) $10 \div 2$, $12 \div 2$

(C) $18 \div 3$, $27 \div 3$ (D) $4 \div 2$, $6 \div 3$

18. Zero divided by any number will give the answer as _______.

(A) zero   (B) one

(C) infinity   (D) none of these

19. If the given number ends with 0, we can not divide the numbers by:

(A) 10   (B) 2

(C) 3   (D) 5

20. $24 \div 6 : 2$ groups of $2 : : 18 \div 2 : ?$

(A) 2 groups of 2   (B) 3 groups of 3

(C) 2 groups of 3   (D) 3 groups of 2

21. In a school there were 2349 pupils. 251 new pupils were admitted into the school and 169 pupils left the school during the year. How many pupils were there in the school at the end of that year?
    (A) 3486
    (B) 2600
    (C) 2431
    (D) 2180

22. Choose the correct option:
    (A) $371 > 231$
    (B) $591 < 326$
    (C) $140 > 200$
    (D) $529 = 226$

23. Golu is 25 years old. His brother Ankit is 4 years elder to him. How old is Ankit?
    A. 21 years
    B. 29 years
    C. 22 years
    D. 24 years

24. Kusum reads 35 page of a book in one day. How many pages can she read in 3 days?
    (A) 100
    (B) 105
    (C) 104
    (D) 108

25. Class 2 students of a school go for a trip. The teacher takes 15 girls and 35 boys to a museum. How many tickets will they need to buy?
    (A) 47 tickets
    (B) 48 tickets
    (C) 49 tickets
    (D) 50 tickets

Darken Your Choice with HB Pencil

	A	B	C	D		A	B	C	D		A	B	C	D		A	B	C	D		A	B	C	D
1.	Ⓐ	Ⓑ	Ⓒ	Ⓓ	6.	Ⓐ	Ⓑ	Ⓒ	Ⓓ	11.	Ⓐ	Ⓑ	Ⓒ	Ⓓ	16.	Ⓐ	Ⓑ	Ⓒ	Ⓓ	21.	Ⓐ	Ⓑ	Ⓒ	Ⓓ
2.	Ⓐ	Ⓑ	Ⓒ	Ⓓ	7.	Ⓐ	Ⓑ	Ⓒ	Ⓓ	12.	Ⓐ	Ⓑ	Ⓒ	Ⓓ	17.	Ⓐ	Ⓑ	Ⓒ	Ⓓ	22.	Ⓐ	Ⓑ	Ⓒ	Ⓓ
3.	Ⓐ	Ⓑ	Ⓒ	Ⓓ	8.	Ⓐ	Ⓑ	Ⓒ	Ⓓ	13.	Ⓐ	Ⓑ	Ⓒ	Ⓓ	18.	Ⓐ	Ⓑ	Ⓒ	Ⓓ	23.	Ⓐ	Ⓑ	Ⓒ	Ⓓ
4.	Ⓐ	Ⓑ	Ⓒ	Ⓓ	9.	Ⓐ	Ⓑ	Ⓒ	Ⓓ	14.	Ⓐ	Ⓑ	Ⓒ	Ⓓ	19.	Ⓐ	Ⓑ	Ⓒ	Ⓓ	24.	Ⓐ	Ⓑ	Ⓒ	Ⓓ
5.	Ⓐ	Ⓑ	Ⓒ	Ⓓ	10.	Ⓐ	Ⓑ	Ⓒ	Ⓓ	15.	Ⓐ	Ⓑ	Ⓒ	Ⓓ	20.	Ⓐ	Ⓑ	Ⓒ	Ⓓ	25.	Ⓐ	Ⓑ	Ⓒ	Ⓓ

FRACTIONS

LEARNING OBJECTIVES

➤ Properties of Fraction
➤ Equivalent Fraction

➤ Types of Fraction

MULTIPLE CHOICE QUESTIONS

1. If the fractions N/6 and 2/3 are equivalent, what is the value of N?

   (A) $N = 2$

   (B) $N = 1$

   (C) $N = 4$

   (D) $N = 3$

2. Which two figures have shaded parts that represent equivalent fractions?

   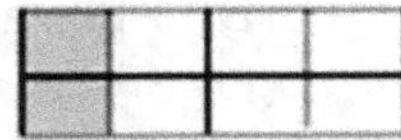
   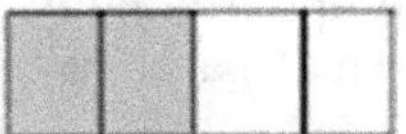

   (A)

   (B)

   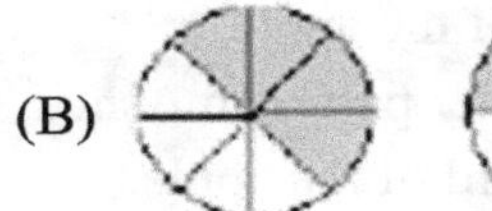

   (C)

   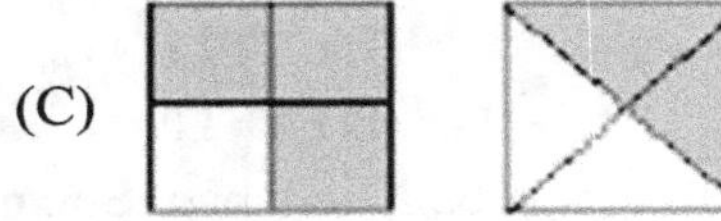

   (D)

   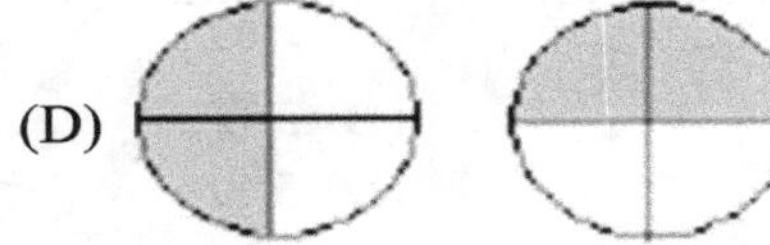

3. Order the following fractions from greatest to least.

   (A) 1/2, 1/3, 1/6, 1/7

   (B) 1/7, 1/6, 1/3, 1/2

   (C) 1/2, 1/6, 1/3, 1/7

   (D) 1/7, 1/2, 1/3, 1/6

4. What value of N makes N/3 < 1/2?

   (A) $N = 3$

   (B) $N = 2$

   (C) $N = 1$

   (D) $N = 4$

5. $\dfrac{1}{4} : \dfrac{2}{8} :: \dfrac{1}{3} : ?$

   (A) $\dfrac{3}{6}$　　　　(B) $\dfrac{2}{6}$

   (C) $\dfrac{3}{9}$　　　　(D) $\dfrac{2}{3}$

6. $\dfrac{3}{4} : \dfrac{4}{3} :: \dfrac{2}{5} : ?$

   (A) $\dfrac{5}{2}$　　　　(B) $\dfrac{2}{10}$

   (C) $\dfrac{5}{10}$　　　　(D) $\dfrac{3}{10}$

7. $\dfrac{1}{2} : \dfrac{1}{4} :: \dfrac{1}{5} : ?$

(A) $\dfrac{1}{8}$ (B) $\dfrac{1}{10}$

(C) $\dfrac{1}{15}$ (D) $\dfrac{1}{6}$

8. How many hours are there in ½ of a day?
   (A) 6 hours
   (B) 12 hours
   (C) 18 hours
   (D) 10 hours

9. How many months are there in ¼ of a year?
   (A) 2 months
   (B) 4 months
   (C) 3 months
   (D) 6 months

10. If you add $\dfrac{1}{2}$ to itself, you will get ______.

   (A) 2   (B) 0
   (C) 1   (D) 4

11. A piece of paper is divided into 5 equal parts. If 3 parts are taken, then fraction for this 3 parts is ________.

   (A) $\dfrac{5}{2}$ (B) $\dfrac{5}{3}$

   (C) $\dfrac{2}{5}$ (D) $\dfrac{3}{5}$

12. Fill the box with correct option.

$$\dfrac{1}{8} + \dfrac{2}{8} = \dfrac{\Box}{8}$$

   (A) 3
   (B) 5
   (C) 6
   (D) 8

13. Three one-third make ________.
   (A) 6
   (B) 3
   (C) 1
   (D) 0

14. Write the fraction for the unshaded part.

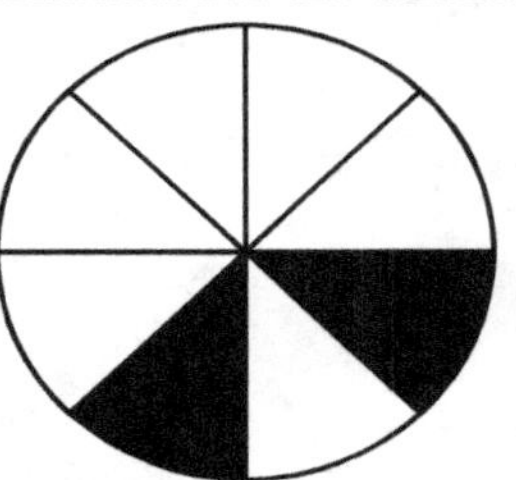

(A) $\dfrac{2}{8}$ (B) $\dfrac{6}{8}$

(C) $\dfrac{5}{8}$ (D) $\dfrac{8}{8}$

15. Write the fraction where numerator is greater than denominator by 3 and sum of numerator and denominator is 9.

(A) $\dfrac{1}{9}$ (B) $\dfrac{2}{5}$

(C) $\dfrac{4}{5}$ (D) $\dfrac{6}{3}$

16. Shraddha, Ashima, Swati and Priya bought 2 pizzas of the same size. Shraddha ate 2/4 of a pizza. Ashima, Swati and Priya ate 1/4 of a pizza each. How much pizza was left?
   (A) 1/4 of a pizza   (B) 1 pizza
   (C) 1/2 of a pizza   (D) 3/4 of a pizza

17. Golu, Ankit and Ashu bought an apple they wanted to share the apple equally. They cut the apple in three equal parts. Which of the following statements are true?
   i.   They all get 1/3 of the apple.
   ii. Ankit gets a smaller part than Ashu.
   iii. Golu gets one-third of the apple.
   iv. Ankit gets one-fourth of the apple.
   (A) TTFF   (B) TTTF
   (C) FFFT   (D) TFTF

18. Shraddha had 5 blue balls in a bag. She put 3 more red ball in the bag. What fraction of the balls were red?
   (A) 3/5   (B) 3/8
   (C) 2/5   (D) 5/8

19. There are 12 people standing in a queue at a ticket counter. One-fourth of the people in the queue are women. How many women are standing?
   (A) 3 women
   (B) 4 women
   (C) 2 women
   (D) 6 women

20. There are 10 birds on a branch of tree. One-fifth of the birds flew away. How many birds are left on the branch?
   (A) 5 birds
   (B) 2 birds
   (C) 8 birds
   (D) 6 birds

HOTS (ACHIEVERS SECTION)

21. A pizza was cut into 8 equal pieces. Kusum ate 3 pieces. What fraction of the pizza is left with her?
   (A) 3/8
   (B) 4/8
   (C) 5/8
   (D) 3/4

22. Which two fractions are equivalent?
   (A) 1/2 and 1/3
   (B) 6/2 and 12/4
   (C) 1/4 and 1/6
   (D) 2/3 and 1/3

23. Shubhra got 4 pastries. She served 2 of them to the guests and kept the remaining in the refrigerator. What fraction of pastries are kept in refrigerator?
   (A) $\dfrac{1}{4}$
   (B) $\dfrac{3}{4}$
   (C) $\dfrac{1}{3}$
   (D) $\dfrac{1}{2}$

24. David completes $\dfrac{2}{3}$ of the total number of questions in maths test paper in 30 minutes. Peter completes $\dfrac{1}{3}$ of the same paper in the same time. Who is faster than other?
   (A) Peter
   (B) David
   (C) Both are equally faster
   (D) All of these

25. Which of the following options represent shaded fraction $7\dfrac{1}{10}$?
   (A)
   (B)
   (C)
   (D)

	A B C D		A B C D		A B C D		A B C D		A B C D
1.	Ⓐ Ⓑ Ⓒ Ⓓ	6.	Ⓐ Ⓑ Ⓒ Ⓓ	11.	Ⓐ Ⓑ Ⓒ Ⓓ	16.	Ⓐ Ⓑ Ⓒ Ⓓ	21.	Ⓐ Ⓑ Ⓒ Ⓓ
2.	Ⓐ Ⓑ Ⓒ Ⓓ	7.	Ⓐ Ⓑ Ⓒ Ⓓ	12.	Ⓐ Ⓑ Ⓒ Ⓓ	17.	Ⓐ Ⓑ Ⓒ Ⓓ	22.	Ⓐ Ⓑ Ⓒ Ⓓ
3.	Ⓐ Ⓑ Ⓒ Ⓓ	8.	Ⓐ Ⓑ Ⓒ Ⓓ	13.	Ⓐ Ⓑ Ⓒ Ⓓ	18.	Ⓐ Ⓑ Ⓒ Ⓓ	23.	Ⓐ Ⓑ Ⓒ Ⓓ
4.	Ⓐ Ⓑ Ⓒ Ⓓ	9.	Ⓐ Ⓑ Ⓒ Ⓓ	14.	Ⓐ Ⓑ Ⓒ Ⓓ	19.	Ⓐ Ⓑ Ⓒ Ⓓ	24.	Ⓐ Ⓑ Ⓒ Ⓓ
5.	Ⓐ Ⓑ Ⓒ Ⓓ	10.	Ⓐ Ⓑ Ⓒ Ⓓ	15.	Ⓐ Ⓑ Ⓒ Ⓓ	20.	Ⓐ Ⓑ Ⓒ Ⓓ	25.	Ⓐ Ⓑ Ⓒ Ⓓ

MONEY

LEARNING OBJECTIVES

➤ Important Facts about Money

MULTIPLE CHOICE QUESTIONS

1. If Ajay wants to buy one pencil and two chocolates, how much he needs to pay?
   (A) ₹15 (B) ₹16.50
   (C) ₹17 (D) ₹17.75

2. Four chocolates can be bought for ₹30 and two pencils can be bought for ₹5. This statement is ________.
   (A) True
   (B) False
   (C) Insufficient information
   (D) None of these

3. Ajay has a five hundred rupees note. He wants to buy as many clocks as he can with this amount. How many clocks can he buy?
   (A) 1 (B) 2
   (C) 3 (D) 4

4. Which of the following statements is not true?
   (A) Cost of (2 banana + 1 pencil) > Cost of 1 chocolate
   (B) Cost of (1 banana + 1 pencil) < Cost of 1 chocolate
   (C) Cost of (1 banana + 2 pencils) > Cost of 1 chocolate
   (D) Cost of (2 bananas + 2 pencils) > Cost of 2 chocolates

5. Calculate the total value of the combination of money.
   ₹5, ₹10, ₹20, ₹50, ₹500, 50 p, 25 p
   (A) ₹600.25
   (B) ₹550.75
   (C) ₹480.50
   (D) ₹585.75

6. Calculate the total value of the combination of money.
   ₹10, ₹10, ₹5, ₹1, ₹2, ₹50, ₹100
   (A) ₹175
   (B) ₹80
   (C) ₹178
   (D) ₹115

7. Arrange the following amounts of money in ascending order:
   ₹2.75 ₹1.75 ₹2.25 ₹2.50 ₹1.50 ₹0.75
   (A) ₹0.75 < ₹1.50 < ₹1.75 < ₹2.50 < ₹2.25 < ₹2.75
   (B) ₹1.75 < ₹1.50 < ₹0.75 < ₹2.25 < ₹2.50 < ₹2.75
   (C) ₹0.75 < ₹1.50 < ₹1.75 < ₹2.25 < ₹2.50 < ₹2.75
   (D) ₹0.75 < ₹1.75 < ₹1.50 < ₹2.25 < ₹2.50 < ₹2.75

8. Arrange the following amounts of money in descending order:

₹10.75, ₹10.65, ₹11.25, ₹11.05, ₹12.50, ₹ 10.55

(A) ₹12.50 > ₹11.25 > ₹11.05 > ₹10.75 > ₹10.65 > ₹10.55

(B) ₹12.50 > ₹11.05 > ₹11.25 > ₹10.75 > ₹10.65> ₹10.55

(C) ₹12.50 > ₹11.25 > ₹11.05 > ₹10.55 > ₹10.65 > ₹10.75

(D) ₹12.50 > ₹11.25 > ₹11.05 > ₹10.65 > ₹10.75 > ₹10.55

9. Read the table:

Item	Cost of each item
Burger	₹10
Book	₹50
Eraser	₹5
Ball	₹6

If you have 150 rupees, how much money will be left with you on buying 2 burgers, 5 balls, 1 book, and 2 erasers.

(A) ₹40   (B) ₹50

(C) ₹10   (D) ₹20

10. 1 Jeans = ₹50

16 Jeans = ________

(A) ₹800

(B) ₹80

(C) ₹1000

(D) ₹500

11. Which of the following sets of notes has least value?

(A)

(B)

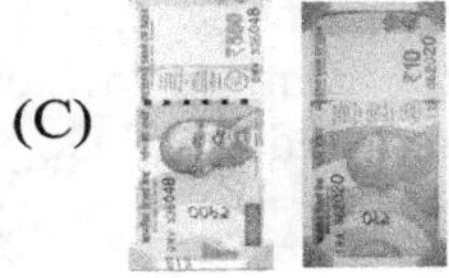

(C)

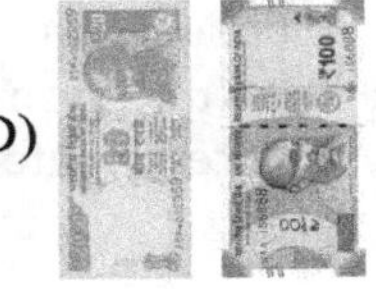

(D)

12. How many paisa are there in ₹5 ________.

(A) 50 paisa

(B) 500 paisa

(C) 5000 paisa

(D) None of these

13. ₹505 and 5 paisa is written as ________.

(A) ₹5055

(B) ₹505.5

(C) ₹50.55

(D) ₹505.05

14. 875 p ☐ ₹8.75

(A) >

(B) <

(C) =

(D) None of these

15. 6p = ________

(A) ₹6

(B) ₹0.06

(C) ₹0.60

(D) ₹.66

16. Raju earned ₹5 everyday during September. How much money did he earn in the whole month?

(A) ₹200

(B) ₹180

(C) ₹150

(D) ₹70

17. Ankita earned ₹2750 for helping her mother in doing house hold chores. She spent ₹950. How much she is left with?

(A) ₹2150

(B) ₹1800

(C) ₹2000

(D) ₹3100

18. Monu wants to purchase books and gave following money to cashier. Four coins of ₹2, two notes of ₹20, three notes of ₹100. If the price of books were ₹326, how much change will he get back?
   (A) ₹20
   (B) ₹22
   (C) ₹25
   (D) ₹28

19. Shraddha bought 6 chocolates. All the chocolates were of the same price. The total cost was ₹88.50. How much money did each chocolate cost?
   (A) 14 rupees
   (B) 14 rupees and 5 paise
   (C) 14 rupees and 50 paise
   (D) 14 rupees and 75 paise

20. If Shubhra bought oranges for ₹75 and she paid ₹100 to fruit seller, which expression shows the correct amount of change that she will get back?
   (A) 100 + 75
   (B) 100 − 75
   (C) 100/75
   (D) 100 × 75

HOTS (ACHIEVERS SECTION)

Direction (1-4): Consider the following story to answer the question.

Raj and his family (his father, mother and sister) went to summer vacation by a plane to an island. Age of Raj is 5 years and his sister is 1 year old. If the fare of flight is as follows:

For two adults one side fare: ₹5000

For 5–15 years old, one side fare: ₹2000

For less than 5 years old, one side fare: ₹500

They stayed in hotel for 4 days for which one day stays was ₹1000. Next morning they went for shopping in which his mother spent ₹5000 for clothing, his father spend ₹2000 to purchase a watch. Raj spent ₹100 on cookies. On second day, Raj and his father went for surfing for which charges were ₹1000 per person.

1. How much total money they spend on flight fare both the sides?
   (A) ₹12500
   (B) ₹15000
   (C) ₹30000
   (D) ₹5000

2. Find the amount spend for stay in the Hotel alone.
   (A) ₹1000
   (B) ₹2000
   (C) ₹3000
   (D) ₹4000

3. What is the total amount they spend on Raj's sister?
   (A) ₹500
   (B) ₹1000
   (C) ₹2000
   (D) ₹3000

4. The total amount spend on shopping is _______ .
   (A) ₹7100
   (B) ₹7200
   (C) ₹7000
   (D) None of these

5. Consider the following scenario to answer the questions. Nikhil went to watch a cricket match in the stadium. He had

₹800 with him. He paid ₹200 for the ticket and a cap for ₹50. Inside the stadium he bought a cold drink for ₹20. At the end of match, he donated ₹50 to the charity club maintained by stadium officials. How much money is left with Nikhil now?

(A) ₹480

(B) ₹320

(C) ₹580

(D) ₹450

-Darken Your Choice with HB Pencil-

1.	Ⓐ Ⓑ Ⓒ Ⓓ	6.	Ⓐ Ⓑ Ⓒ Ⓓ	11.	Ⓐ Ⓑ Ⓒ Ⓓ	16.	Ⓐ Ⓑ Ⓒ Ⓓ	21.	Ⓐ Ⓑ Ⓒ Ⓓ
2.	Ⓐ Ⓑ Ⓒ Ⓓ	7.	Ⓐ Ⓑ Ⓒ Ⓓ	12.	Ⓐ Ⓑ Ⓒ Ⓓ	17.	Ⓐ Ⓑ Ⓒ Ⓓ	22.	Ⓐ Ⓑ Ⓒ Ⓓ
3.	Ⓐ Ⓑ Ⓒ Ⓓ	8.	Ⓐ Ⓑ Ⓒ Ⓓ	13.	Ⓐ Ⓑ Ⓒ Ⓓ	18.	Ⓐ Ⓑ Ⓒ Ⓓ	23.	Ⓐ Ⓑ Ⓒ Ⓓ
4.	Ⓐ Ⓑ Ⓒ Ⓓ	9.	Ⓐ Ⓑ Ⓒ Ⓓ	14.	Ⓐ Ⓑ Ⓒ Ⓓ	19.	Ⓐ Ⓑ Ⓒ Ⓓ	24.	Ⓐ Ⓑ Ⓒ Ⓓ
5.	Ⓐ Ⓑ Ⓒ Ⓓ	10.	Ⓐ Ⓑ Ⓒ Ⓓ	15.	Ⓐ Ⓑ Ⓒ Ⓓ	20.	Ⓐ Ⓑ Ⓒ Ⓓ	25.	Ⓐ Ⓑ Ⓒ Ⓓ

LENGTH, WEIGHT, CAPACITY & TIME

LEARNING OBJECTIVES

- ➤ Measuring Tapes
- ➤ Rulers/Measuring Tapes
- ➤ Measuring Weight
- ➤ Capacity and Volume
- ➤ Time
- ➤ Calendar

MULTIPLE CHOICE QUESTIONS

Direction (1–2): Read the table given below and answer the questions that follows:

No.	Name of dress	Length of cloth required
i.	Frock	4 metres
ii.	Skirt	3 metres
iii.	Shorts	125 centimetres
iv.	Kurti	250 centimetres
v.	Jeans	2 metres

1. Which dress requires minimum length of cloth?
   (A) Skirt
   (B) Shorts
   (C) Kurti
   (D) Jeans

2. Which of the following statement is correct?
   A: Kurti needs more cloth than jeans.
   B: Shorts needs more cloth than skirt.
   C: Frock dose not needs more cloth than skirt.
   D: Jeans needs less cloth than frock.
   (A) B
   (B) C
   (C) D
   (D) A

3. Thing which can be measured in centimetres is _______.
   (A) Length of street pole
   (B) Height of a water tank
   (C) Width of T.V.
   (D) Length of kurta

4. Thing which cannot be measured in metres is _______.
   (A) Depth of a ocean
   (B) Height of a tree
   (C) Height of a cat
   (D) Distance in a room

Directions (5): Choose the correct option from the following:

5. The standard unit of length is _______.
   (A) metre
   (B) kilometre
   (C) decimetre
   (D) decametre

6. 1. Pineapple
   2. Cherry
   3. Mango
   4. Chikoo

(A) 1342

(B) 3142

(C) 3124

(D) 1324

Direction (7–8): Read the table below and answer the questions that below:

S. No.	Items	Weight
1	Wheat flour	More than 1 kg
2	Sugar	More than 1 kg
3	Butter	Less than 1 kg
4	Ghee	1kg
5	Curd	Less than 1 kg
6	Oil	1 kg

7. Sugar : Wheat Flour :: ? : Oil

(A) Butter

(B) Ghee

(C) Curd

(D) Sugar

8. Butter : Less than 1 kg :: ? : more than 1 kg.

(A) Oil

(B) Ghee

(C) Wheat Flour

(D) Curd

Directions (9–10): Read the following table and answer the questions that follow:

Weight	Rate
0–5kg	₹20
6–10 kg	₹40
11–20 kg	₹60
21–30 kg	₹80

9. How many 7 kg pumpin cost?

(A) ₹20

(B) ₹40

(C) ₹60

(D) ₹80

10. How much 12000 gm pumpkin cost?

(A) ₹20

(B) ₹40

(C) ₹60

(D) ₹80

11. If 2540 ml : 2 L 540 ml :: ? : : 1 L 5 ml

(A) 1050 ml

(B) 1500 ml

(C) 5001 ml

(D) 1005 ml

12. If 3 L 69 ml : 3069 l : : ? : 3020 ml

(A) 3 L 20 ml

(B) 3 L 200 ml

(C) 3 L 2 ml

(D) 3 L 2000 ml

13. How many buckets of water are needed to fill the water cooler of capacity 45 L? The capacity of a bucket is 5 L.

(A) 6

(B) 7

(C) 8

(D) 9

14. I collected different containers and started thinking about their capacities. I wrote few sentences about them. Write true/false for the sentences I wrote.

A: A cup can hold more coffee than a saucepan.

B: A spoon can hold less sugar than a bowl.

C: A glass can hold more water than a bottle.

D: A saucepan can hold more tea than a cup.

(A) FFFT

(B) TFFT

(C) FTFT

(D) FFFF

15. I had 1L of oil. After using the oil for the recipies I was left with 175 ml of oil. How much did I use for the recipies?
    (A) 625 ml
    (B) 725 ml
    (C) 825 ml
    (D) 925 ml

16. Noon time refers to __________.
    (A) 12 pm
    (B) 12 am
    (C) 11:55 pm
    (D) 11:55 am

17. How much times is there between 9:30 am and 11:00am?
    (A) 1 hour
    (B) 1 hour 15 minutes
    (C) 1 hour 30 minutes
    (D) 2 hours

18. What is the ideal lunch time?
    (A) 2:00 pm   (B) 5:00 pm
    (C) 8:00 am   (D) 8:00 pm

19. What time is referred as midnight?
    (A) 12 am   (B) 12 pm
    (C) 1 pm   (D) 2 am

20. Which month of the year has the least number of days?
    (A) January   (B) July
    (C) May   (D) February

21. Anita goes for jogging early in the morning. She takes 2 rounds everyday around the park. She jogs a distance of 2 km every day. Anita states the following four statements. State true or False.
    A. "One round of the park is 1 km."
    B. "I jog 2000 m every day."
    C. "I jog 200 m every day."
    D. "3 rounds of the park will be 300 m."
    (A) TTFF
    (B) TFTF
    (C) FFFT
    (d) FFTT

22. Bunny was watching National Geogra-phic channel and saw different animals. He started thinking about their weights and noted about them a paper. There were some mistakes in his estimate. Find the mistake and choose the correct option based on true or false.
    1. Weight of elephant is more than 1000 kg.
    2. Weight of a big snake is less than 10 kg.
    3. Weight of a fox is less than 50 kg.
    4. Weight of lion is more than 200 kg.
    (A) TFTF
    (B) FTFT
    (C) FTTF
    (D) TFFT

23. Rancho wants to fill a kettle (1 It), bowl (750 ml) and a bottle (500 ml) with water. He has a glass (250 ml) with him. Can you estimate the number of glasses of water he needs to fill a kettle?
    (A) 2
    (B) 3
    (C) 4
    (D) 5

24. The first session of a cricket match began at 8 : 15 A.M. It lasted 3 hours and 30 minutes. What time did the first session end?

(A) 8 : 45 A.M.

(B) 10 : 45 A.M.

(C) 12 : 45 P.M.

(D) 11 : 45 A.M.

25. Madhu's party started at 6:30 P.M. and ended at 9 : 00 P.M.

What was the total amount of time that Madhu's party lasted?

(A) 2 hours

(B) 2 hours 30 min

(C) 3 hours

(D) 3 hours 30 min

1.	Ⓐ	Ⓑ	Ⓒ	Ⓓ	6.	Ⓐ	Ⓑ	Ⓒ	Ⓓ	11.	Ⓐ	Ⓑ	Ⓒ	Ⓓ	16.	Ⓐ	Ⓑ	Ⓒ	Ⓓ	21.	Ⓐ	Ⓑ	Ⓒ Ⓓ
2.	Ⓐ	Ⓑ	Ⓒ	Ⓓ	7.	Ⓐ	Ⓑ	Ⓒ	Ⓓ	12.	Ⓐ	Ⓑ	Ⓒ	Ⓓ	17.	Ⓐ	Ⓑ	Ⓒ	Ⓓ	22.	Ⓐ	Ⓑ	Ⓒ Ⓓ
3.	Ⓐ	Ⓑ	Ⓒ	Ⓓ	8.	Ⓐ	Ⓑ	Ⓒ	Ⓓ	13.	Ⓐ	Ⓑ	Ⓒ	Ⓓ	18.	Ⓐ	Ⓑ	Ⓒ	Ⓓ	23.	Ⓐ	Ⓑ	Ⓒ Ⓓ
4.	Ⓐ	Ⓑ	Ⓒ	Ⓓ	9.	Ⓐ	Ⓑ	Ⓒ	Ⓓ	14.	Ⓐ	Ⓑ	Ⓒ	Ⓓ	19.	Ⓐ	Ⓑ	Ⓒ	Ⓓ	24.	Ⓐ	Ⓑ	Ⓒ Ⓓ
5.	Ⓐ	Ⓑ	Ⓒ	Ⓓ	10.	Ⓐ	Ⓑ	Ⓒ	Ⓓ	15.	Ⓐ	Ⓑ	Ⓒ	Ⓓ	20.	Ⓐ	Ⓑ	Ⓒ	Ⓓ	25.	Ⓐ	Ⓑ	Ⓒ Ⓓ

GEOMETRY

6

➤ Plane Figures
➤ Point, Line, Ray

➤ Solid Figures

MULTIPLE CHOICE QUESTIONS

1. What is the shape of centre tile?

   (A) square   (B) oval
   (C) rectangle   (D) triangle

2. What is the shape of tent door?

   (A) circle   (B) square
   (C) rectangle   (D) triangle

3. What is the shape of wheels of the wagon?

   (A) rectangle   (B) triangle
   (C) circle   (D) none of these

4. I am the shape of a license plate. My shape is also found on refrigerators or windows. What am I?
   (A) rectangle
   (B) circle
   (C) square
   (D) triangle

5. I can be found around your yard or even in your bedroom. It's because of me that toys roll and bikes go. I have no sides and no corners. What am I?
   (A) rectangle
   (B) circle
   (C) square
   (D) triangle

6. My shape is used for many things like signs, gift boxes and windows. All my four sides are the same. What am I?
   (A) rectangle   (B) circle
   (C) square   (D) triangle

7. My shape is found on yield signs and on the frames of a bridge. Although I only have three sides, I can be very strong. What am I?
   (A) rectangle
   (B) circle
   (C) square
   (D) triangle

8. Name the shape.

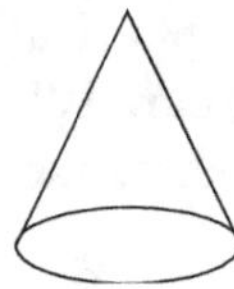

(A) cube
(B) cone
(C) cuboid
(D) cylinder

9. Name the shape.

(A) Rectangle   (B) Triangle
(C) Square   (D) Circle

10. What is the shape of this button?

(A) triangle
(B) square
(C) octagon
(D) circle

11. The figure has __________ triangles.

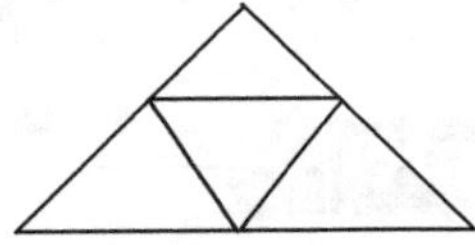

(A) 4   (B) 3
(C) 5   (D) 2

12. The figures has __________ squares.

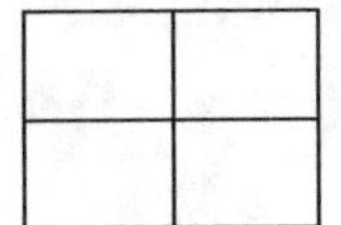

(A) 5   (B) 4
(C) 3   (D) 1

13. How many meeting points are there in a square?

(A) 4
(B) 3
(C) 2
(D) 1

14. How many line segments are there in the given figure?

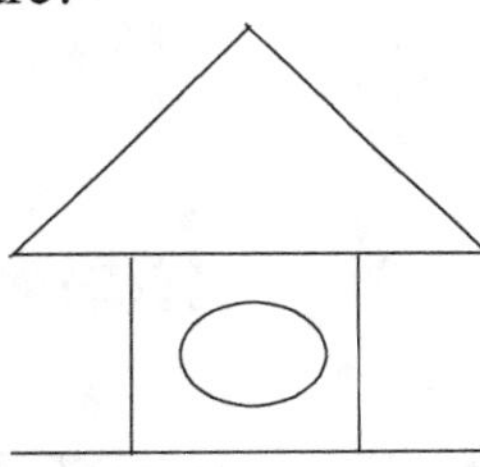

(A) 6
(B) 3
(C) 7
(D) 4

15. Match the columns.

Column I		Column II
A. Square	(i)	(triangle)
B. Rectangle	(ii)	(circle)
C. Triangle	(iii)	(square)
D. Circle	(iv)	(rectangle)

(A) A – i, B – ii, C – iii, D – iv
(B) A – iii, B – iv, C – i, D – ii
(C) A – iii, B – iv, C – ii, D – i
(D) A – ii, B – i, C – iv, D – iii

16. Tarun puts some shapes into a group shown below by considering the rule "all the shapes have four sides".

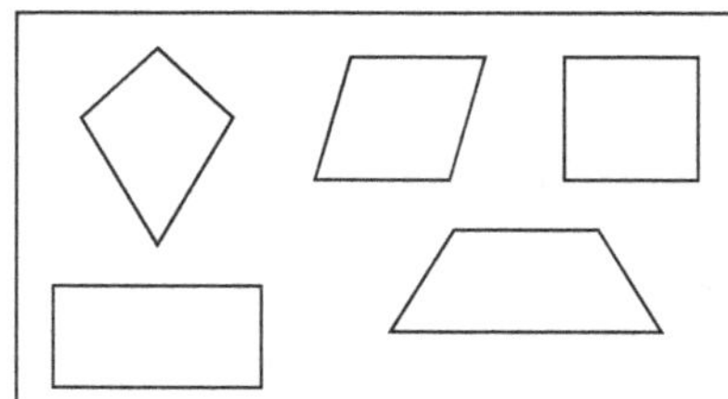

Which shape belongs to his group?

(A) 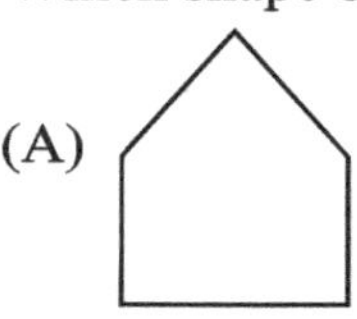

(B) 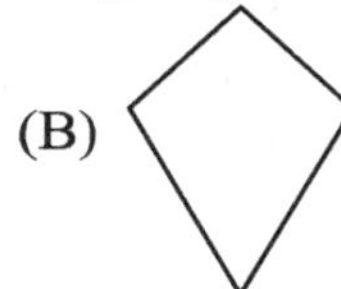

(C) 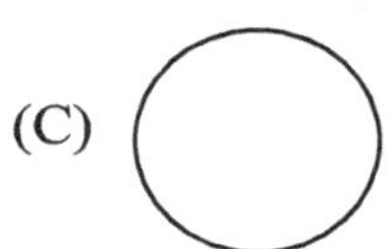

(D) 

17. Aruna wrote about a square but she wrote one wrong statement. Help her out to find out that wrong statement.

Statement (i) All the sides of a square are equal.

Statement (ii) A square has four side.

Statement (iii) A square has three corner.

(A) (i) (B) (ii)

(C) (iii) (D) Both (i) and (ii)

18. Soma has cuboid box, Tanya has cylinderical can, Rohan has spherical ball and Charu has conical birthday cap. Who has the shape with maximum number of faces.

(A) Tanya (B) Soma

(C) Rohan (D) Charu

19. Match the following columns.

	Column I		Column II
A.	Cuboid	i.	Ball
B.	Cube	ii.	Lunch Box
C.	Sphere	iii.	Birthday Cap
D.	Cone	iv.	Dice

   A B C D

(A) ii, i, iv, iii

(B) i, ii, iii, iv

(C) ii, iv, i, iii

(D) ii, iv, iii, i

20. Each of the signs below shows a different kind of road. Which sign of the road has horizontal lines only.

(A) 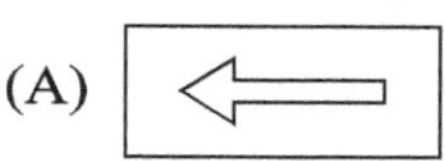

(B) 

(C) 

(D) None of these

HOTS (ACHIEVERS SECTION)

21. Which one is a closed shape?

(A) 

(B) 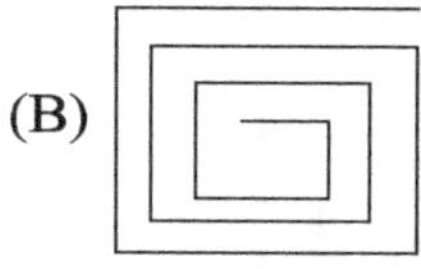

(C) 

(D) 

22. How many straight sides does the circle have?

(A) 0 (B) 1

(C) 2 (D) 3

OLYMPIAD WORKBOOK (IMO) CLASS– 3

23. These shapes have the same number of sides.

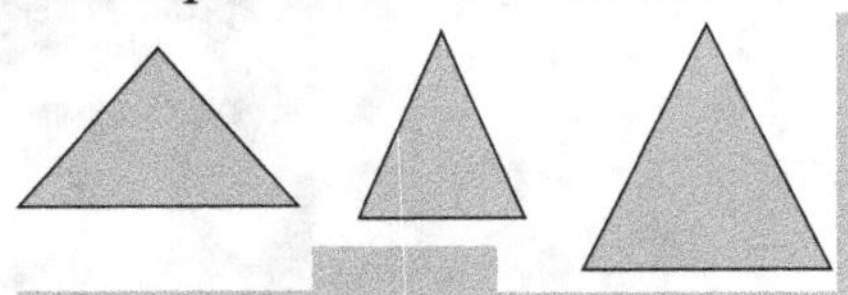

(A) True   (B) False

24. A _____ is bounded by three line segments.

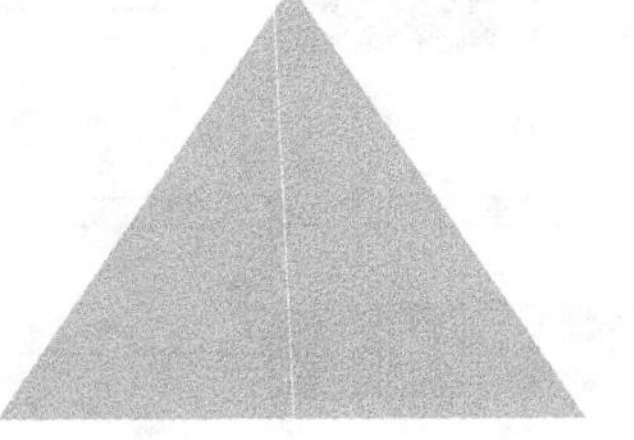

(A) Triangle   (B) Cone
(C) Rectangle   (D) Circle

25. Look at the two shapes. Which of the following is NOT true?

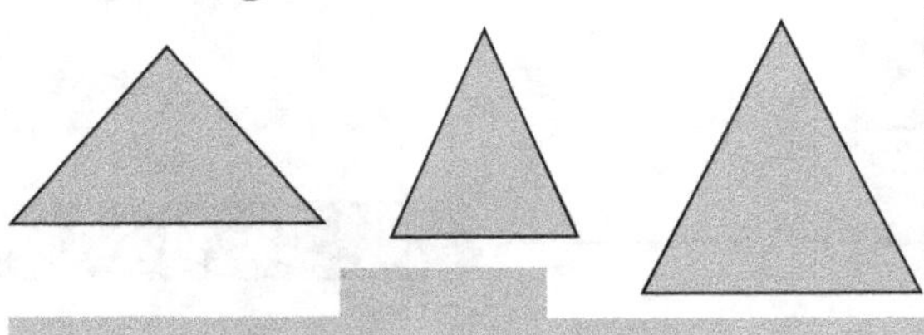

(A) They are all triangles.
(B) They are the same size.
(C) They have the same number of sides.
(D) They have the same number of corners.

---

1. Ⓐ Ⓑ Ⓒ Ⓓ	6. Ⓐ Ⓑ Ⓒ Ⓓ	11. Ⓐ Ⓑ Ⓒ Ⓓ	16. Ⓐ Ⓑ Ⓒ Ⓓ	21. Ⓐ Ⓑ Ⓒ Ⓓ
2. Ⓐ Ⓑ Ⓒ Ⓓ	7. Ⓐ Ⓑ Ⓒ Ⓓ	12. Ⓐ Ⓑ Ⓒ Ⓓ	17. Ⓐ Ⓑ Ⓒ Ⓓ	22. Ⓐ Ⓑ Ⓒ Ⓓ
3. Ⓐ Ⓑ Ⓒ Ⓓ	8. Ⓐ Ⓑ Ⓒ Ⓓ	13. Ⓐ Ⓑ Ⓒ Ⓓ	18. Ⓐ Ⓑ Ⓒ Ⓓ	23. Ⓐ Ⓑ Ⓒ Ⓓ
4. Ⓐ Ⓑ Ⓒ Ⓓ	9. Ⓐ Ⓑ Ⓒ Ⓓ	14. Ⓐ Ⓑ Ⓒ Ⓓ	19. Ⓐ Ⓑ Ⓒ Ⓓ	24. Ⓐ Ⓑ Ⓒ Ⓓ
5. Ⓐ Ⓑ Ⓒ Ⓓ	10. Ⓐ Ⓑ Ⓒ Ⓓ	15. Ⓐ Ⓑ Ⓒ Ⓓ	20. Ⓐ Ⓑ Ⓒ Ⓓ	25. Ⓐ Ⓑ Ⓒ Ⓓ

DATA HANDLING

LEARNING OBJECTIVES

➤ Pictographs ➤ Tally Marks

MULTIPLE CHOICE QUESTIONS

Direction [1-5]: The pictograph shows the number of books read by each student.

Charu	▯▯
Manu	▯▯▯
Rohan	▯▯▯▯
Sahil	▯
Kapil	▯▯

Each ▯ represents 5 books.

1. How many more books did Rohan read than Manu?
   (A) 10
   (B) 1
   (C) 5
   (D) 2

2. What is the total number of books read by all students?
   (A) 70
   (B) 60
   (C) 50
   (D) 40

3. Which student read same number of books?
   (A) Rohan and Kapil
   (B) Manu and Sahil
   (C) Charu and Manu
   (D) Kapil and Charu

4. Who read least number of books?
   (A) Sahil
   (B) Charu
   (C) Manu
   (D) Kapil

5. Who read more book, Manu or Kapil and by how much?
   (A) Kapil, 10
   (B) Manu, 5
   (C) Kapil, 5
   (D) Rohan, 5

Direction [6–10]: The pictograph shows number of students who were absent in a day on a particular week.

Monday	◯◯
Tuesday	◯◯◯◯
Wednesday	◯◯◯
Thursday	◯

Friday	◯ ◯ ◯ ◯	
Saturday	◯ ◯	
Each ◯ means 2 students		

6. On which day 2 students were absent?
   (A) Thursday
   (B) Monday
   (C) Tuesday
   (D) Friday
7. How many students were absent on Monday?
   (A) 4
   (B) 6
   (C) 8
   (D) 5
8. On which day minimum number of students were absent?
   (A) Tuesday
   (B) Monday
   (C) Thursday
   (D) Friday
9. How many students were absent on Friday and Saturday both?
   (A) 6
   (B) 12
   (C) 8
   (D) 10
10. What is the total number of students that absent in the week?
    (A) 32
    (B) 30
    (C) 36
    (D) 27

Direction [16-20]: Read the tally chart that represents different drinks liked by students and answer the questions given below.

Drinks	No. of Students
Apple Juice	卌 IIII
Pepsi	IIII
Coke	I 卌 I 卌 III
Milk	I 卌 I 卌 II

11. What is the most popular drink?
    (A) Apple juice
    (B) Pepsi
    (C) Coke
    (D) Milk
12. How many students chose Pepsi as their favourite drink?
    (A) 14
    (B) 4
    (C) 15
    (D) 12
13. What is the least popular drink?
    (A) Coke
    (B) Apple juice
    (C) Pepsi
    (D) Milk
14. How many students answered the survey?
    (A) 40
    (B) 38
    (C) 45
    (D) 40
15. How many more students chose coke as their favourite drink than those who chose pepsi?
    (A) 2
    (B) 3
    (C) 10
    (D) 9

Direction [15-20]: The tally graph shows the type of coloured pens liked by various children.

Red	ⅢⅠ
Blue	ⅢⅢⅠⅠ
Green	ⅢⅢⅢ
Pink	ⅢⅠ
Black	ⅢⅢⅠⅠ

16. How many more children liked green than red coloured pen?

(A) 5

(B) 10

(C) 15

(D) 20

17. Which coloured pen is liked by maximum number of students?

(A) Green

(B) Red

(C) Blue

(D) Black

18. How many children liked black coloured pen?

(A) 14

(B) 12

(C) 15

(D) 20

19. How many children liked green and black coloured pen altogether?

(A) 15

(B) 25

(C) 30

(D) 27

20. Which coloured pen is least liked by children.

(A) Red and Pink

(B) Green

(C) Blue

(D) None of these

HOTS (ACHIEVERS SECTION)

21. Look at this pictograph and answer the following question.

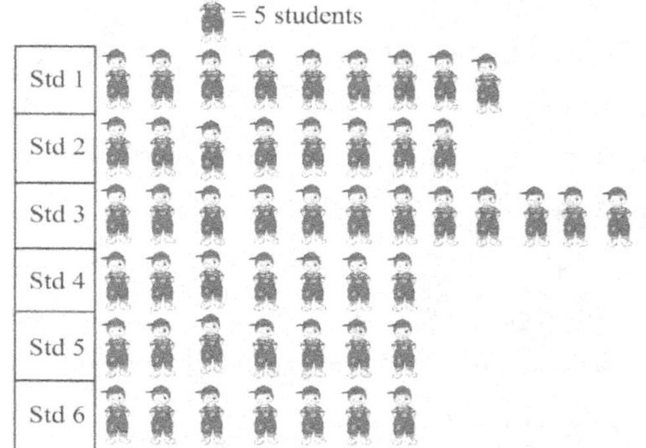

Which class has maximum students?

(A) Class 3

(B) Class 4

(C) Class 5

(D) Class 6

22. This graph shows the different types of clothes in a wardrobe. Look at the graph and answer the following question.

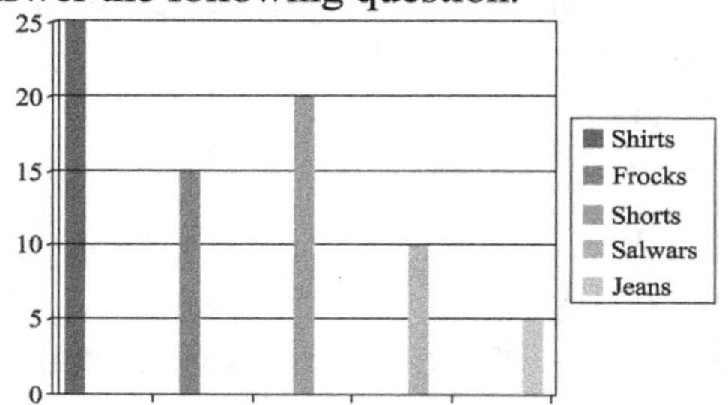

How many salwars are there in the wardrobe?

(A) 10

(B) 5

(C) 12

(D) 26

23. The following graph shows how the employees of a company go for work. Read

the graph and answer the following question.

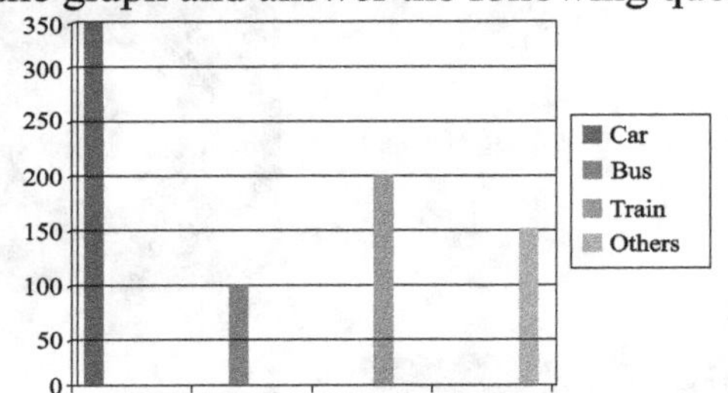

How many employees go for work by train?

(A) 100

(B) 200

(C) 390

(D) 250

24. Use the given pictograph to answer the following questions.

Mode of transport to school–Class III

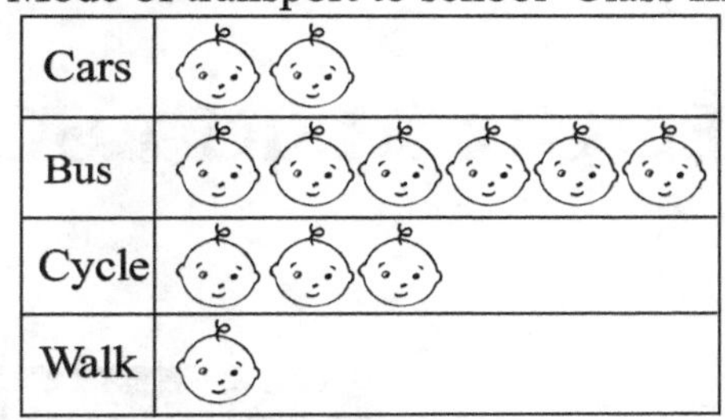

= 10 children

How many more children come by car than by walk?

(A) 10

(B) 20

(C) 30

(D) 40

1.	Ⓐ Ⓑ Ⓒ Ⓓ	6.	Ⓐ Ⓑ Ⓒ Ⓓ	11.	Ⓐ Ⓑ Ⓒ Ⓓ	16.	Ⓐ Ⓑ Ⓒ Ⓓ	21.	Ⓐ Ⓑ Ⓒ Ⓓ
2.	Ⓐ Ⓑ Ⓒ Ⓓ	7.	Ⓐ Ⓑ Ⓒ Ⓓ	12.	Ⓐ Ⓑ Ⓒ Ⓓ	17.	Ⓐ Ⓑ Ⓒ Ⓓ	22.	Ⓐ Ⓑ Ⓒ Ⓓ
3.	Ⓐ Ⓑ Ⓒ Ⓓ	8.	Ⓐ Ⓑ Ⓒ Ⓓ	13.	Ⓐ Ⓑ Ⓒ Ⓓ	18.	Ⓐ Ⓑ Ⓒ Ⓓ	23.	Ⓐ Ⓑ Ⓒ Ⓓ
4.	Ⓐ Ⓑ Ⓒ Ⓓ	9.	Ⓐ Ⓑ Ⓒ Ⓓ	14.	Ⓐ Ⓑ Ⓒ Ⓓ	19.	Ⓐ Ⓑ Ⓒ Ⓓ	24.	Ⓐ Ⓑ Ⓒ Ⓓ
5.	Ⓐ Ⓑ Ⓒ Ⓓ	10.	Ⓐ Ⓑ Ⓒ Ⓓ	15.	Ⓐ Ⓑ Ⓒ Ⓓ	20.	Ⓐ Ⓑ Ⓒ Ⓓ		

LOGICAL REASONING

8

- The Concept of Pattern
- Analogy
- Types of Classification
- Coding and Decoding
- Alphabetical Order
- Word Formation
- Figure Matrix
- The Ranking Test
- Ranking/Position Identification
- Mirror Image
- Embedded Figures
- Days and Dates
- Possible Combinations

MULTIPLE CHOICE QUESTIONS

1. Write the numbers to complete the following table:

IN	18	17	16	15	10	9
OUT	15	14	13			

(A) 10, 8, 6   (B) 4, 6, 8
(C) 12, 7, 6   (D) 12, 8, 4

2. Write the numbers to complete the following table:

IN	28	27	26	25	18	17
OUT	23	22	21			

(A) 10, 8, 6   (B) 4, 6, 8
(C) 6, 10, 14   (D) 20, 13, 12

3. 

(A) 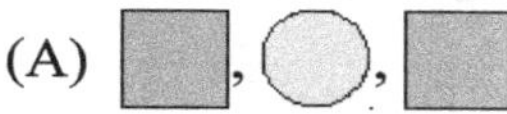

(B) 

(C)

(D)

4.

(A) □, ⬡, □

(B) □, □, ⬡

(C) □, ⬡, ⬡

(D) ⬡, □, ⬡

5.

(A) ○, ○, ⬠

(B) ○, ⬠, ⬠

(C) ⬠, ⬠, ⬠

(D) ○, ⬠, ○

6. A : C :: X : ?

(A) Y   (B) Z

(C) T   (D) U

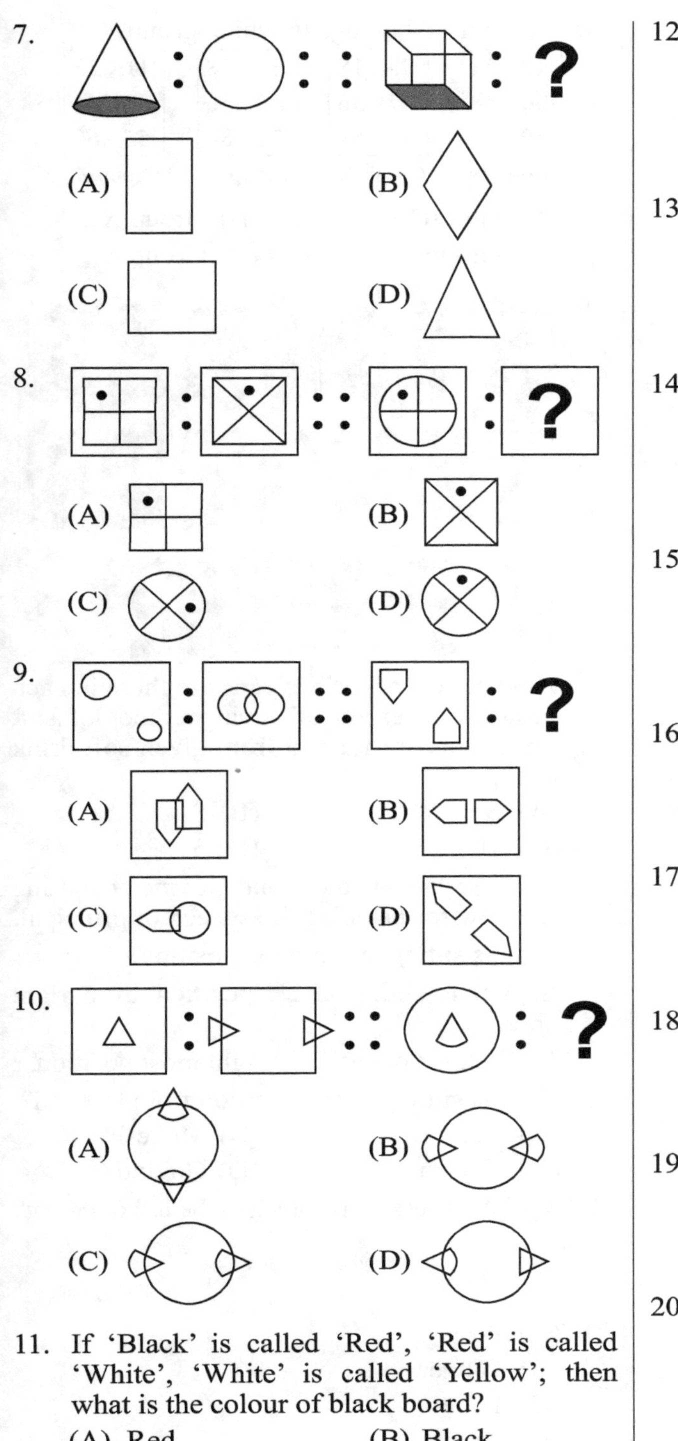

7.

(A) (B) (C) (D)

8.

(A) (B) (C) (D)

9.

(A) (B) (C) (D)

10.

(A) (B) (C) (D)

11. If 'Black' is called 'Red', 'Red' is called 'White', 'White' is called 'Yellow'; then what is the colour of black board?

(A) Red (B) Black
(C) White (D) Yellow

12. If 'Mumbai' is called 'Jaipur', 'Jaipur' is called 'Delhi', 'Delhi' is called 'Lucknow' then what is the capital of India?

(A) Mumbai (B) Delhi
(C) Lucknow (D) Jaipur

13. If 'Policeman' is called 'Postman', 'Postman' is called 'Doctor' 'Doctor' is called 'Teacher' then who does treat people?

(A) Policeman (B) Doctor
(C) Postman (D) Teacher

14. If 'Sheep' is called 'Cow', 'Cow' is called 'Bees', 'Bees' is called 'Tiger', then who gives honey to us?

(A) Sheep (B) Tiger
(C) Bees (D) Cow

15. If 'House' is called 'Nest', 'Nest' is called 'Kennel', Kennel' is called 'Cave'. Where does dog live?

(A) Cave (B) Kennel
(C) Nest (D) House

16. Which letter appears in RESIDENT, but not in REINVEST?

(A) D (B) V
(C) I (D) S

17. Which letter occurs once in FLAG, but twice in APPEARING?

(A) F (B) G
(C) P (D) A

18. Which letter occurs once in EXERCISE, but twice in SUCCESS?

(A) C (B) E
(C) S (D) R

19. Which letter occurs twice as often in POTATOES as it does in SILENT?

(A) E (B) O
(C) T (D) S

20. Arrange the given words in alphabetical order and choose the one that comes first.

Conceive, Diurnal, Conceit, Concentrate

(A) Conceive (B) Diurnal
(C) Conceit (D) Concentrate

21.

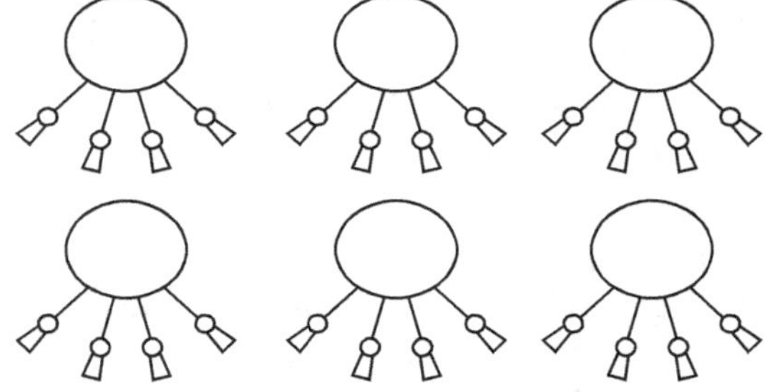

How many bunches of 3 keys can be formed from given bunch of keys.

(A) 5

(B) 7

(C) 6

(D) 8

22.

How many groups of 4 bats can be formed from given bats.

(A) 5   (B) 6

(C) 8   (D) 3

23. Alphabet 'U' belongs to which group?

(A) A, E, I, ...

(B) P, Q, R, ...

(C) X,Y, Z, ...

(D) L, M, N, ...

24. Number 66 belongs to which group?

12, 24	9, 18	14, 28	11, 22
36, 48	27, 36	42, 56	33, 44
60, 72	45, 54	70, 84	55, 66
Group W	Group X	Group Y	Group Z

(A) Group W   (B) Group X

(C) Group Y   (D) Group Z

25.

How many soft drinks cans are there in each group, if z group of equal number of soft drink cans are formed from given soft drink cans?

(A) 6   (B) 8

(C) 10   (D) 5

26. Ram, Shyam, Mukesh and Govind are sitting in a row for listening the speech of principal.

Ram is sitting at left most position.

Shyam is sitting at 2nd position from right end.

Mukesh is not sitting at right most position.

Who is sitting at 2nd position from left end?

(A) Ram   (B) Mukesh

(C) Shyam   (D) Govind

27. Which vegetable is fourth to the left of carrot?

(A) Peas

(B) Ginger

(C) Potato

(D) Onion

OLYMPIAD WORKBOOK (IMO) CLASS— 3

28. If hockey stick is removed from the row, then what is the middle of row?

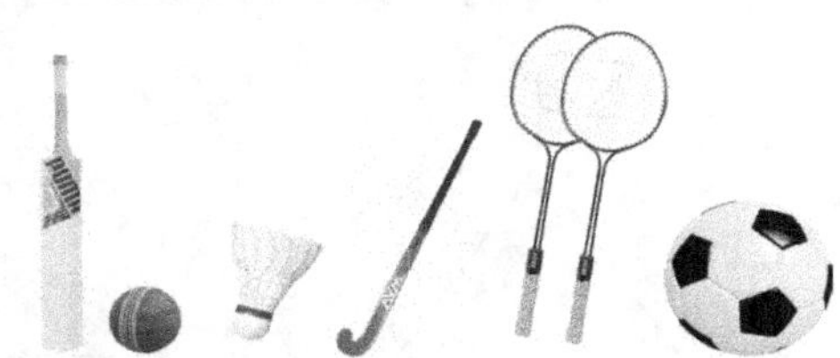

(A) Shuttle   (B) Racket
(C) Ball   (D) Bat

29.

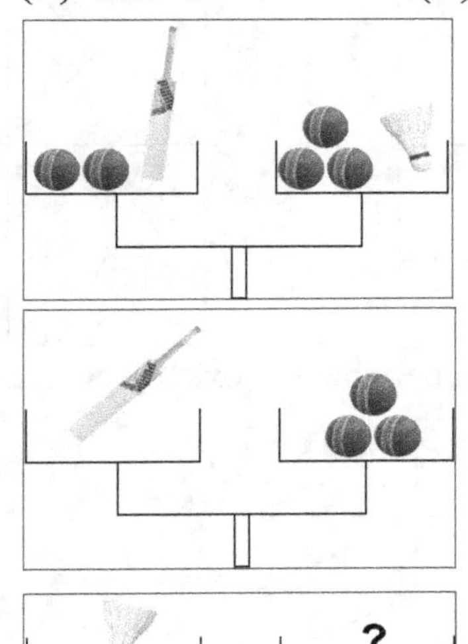

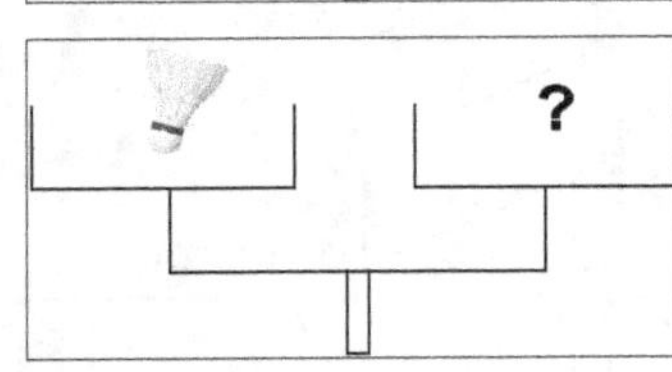

(A) 

(B) 

(C) 

(D)

30. In a row of some students, Ram is second from the left end and fourth from the right end. Find the total number of students.

(A) 10   (B) 5
(C) 7   (D) 8

31.  Mirror

(A) **3**   (B) **Ɛ**

(C) **Ɛ**   (D) **3**

32. 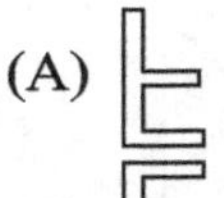 Mirror

(A)

(B)

(C)

(D)

33. Mirror

(A)   (B)

(C)   (D)

34. 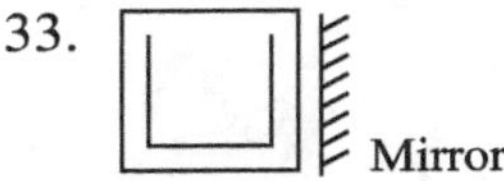 Mirror

(A)

(B)

(C)

(D)

35. 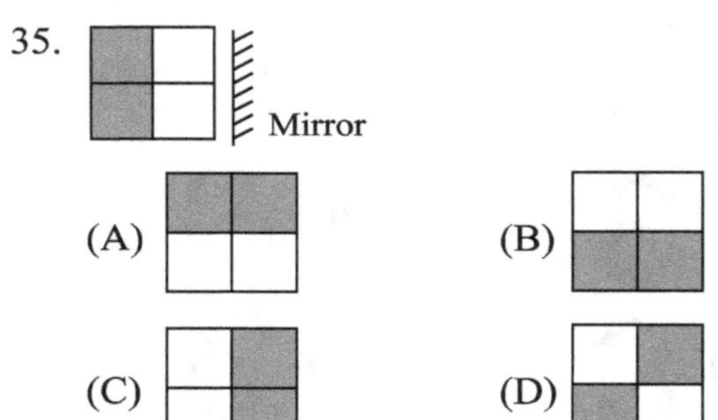

(A)   (B)

(C)   (D)

36. Which of the following shapes is not embedded in figure (Z).

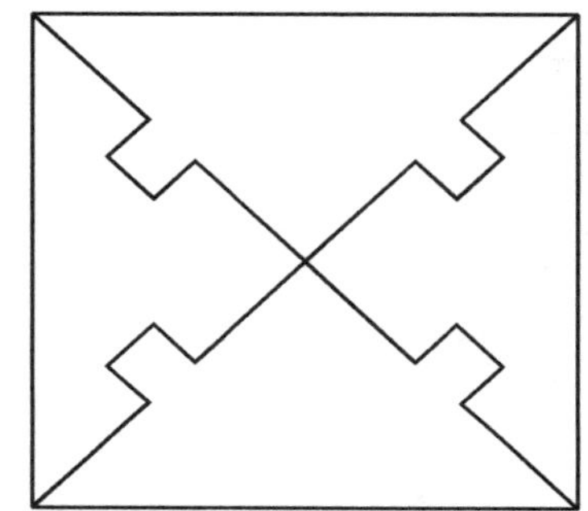

Fig. (Z)

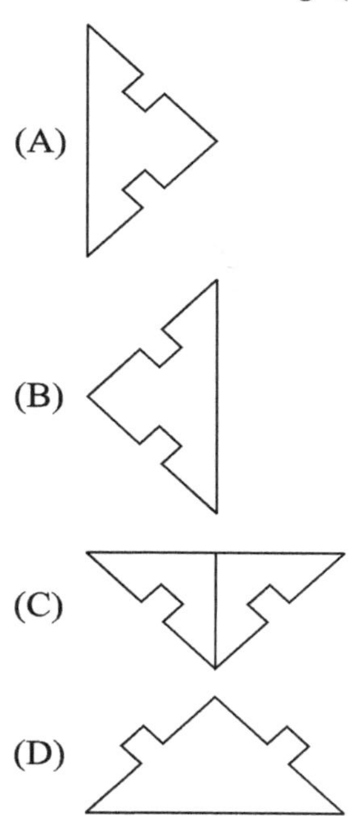

(A)

(B)

(C)

(D)

37. Find the figure from the options in which the figure (Z) is exactly embedded as one of its parts.

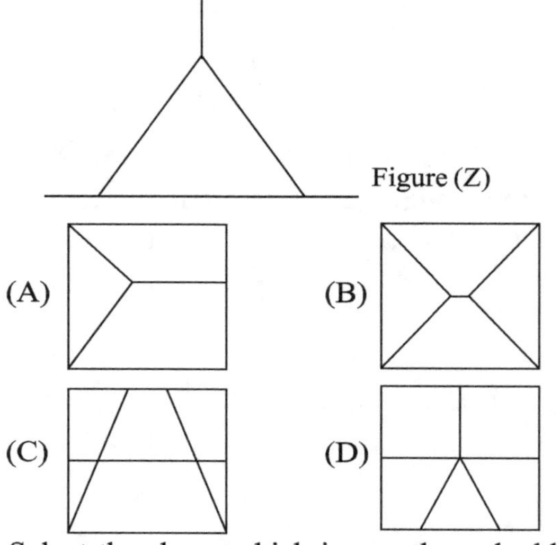

Figure (Z)

(A)   (B)

(C)   (D)

38. Select the shape which is exactly embedded in figure (Z).

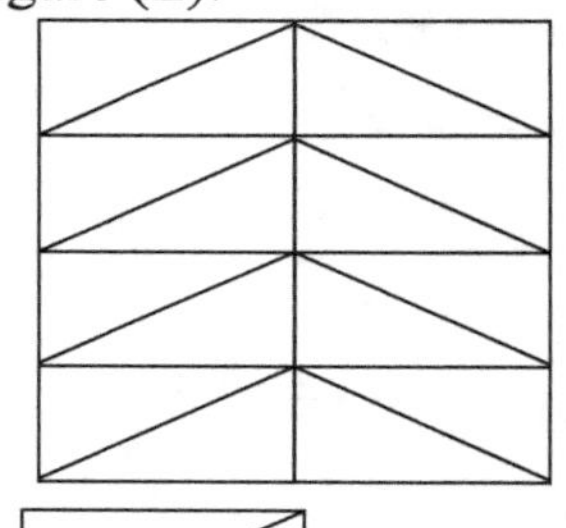

Figure (Z)

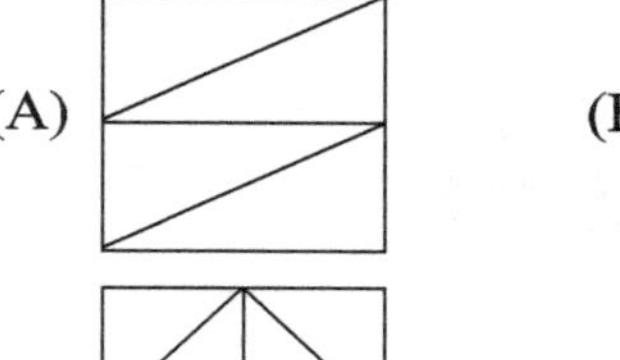
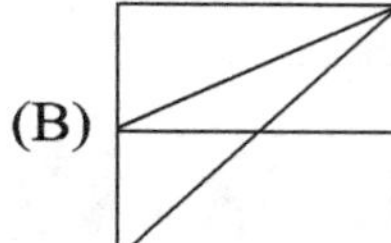

(A)   (B)

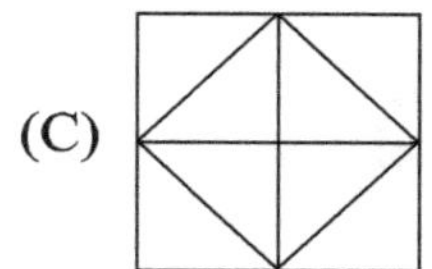
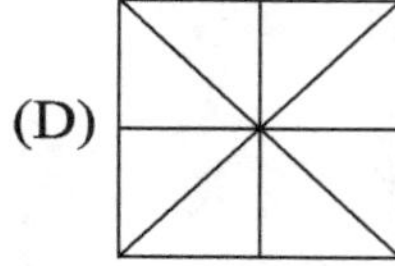

(C)   (D)

39. Find out the alternative figure which contains figure (X) as its part.

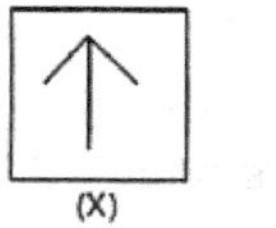
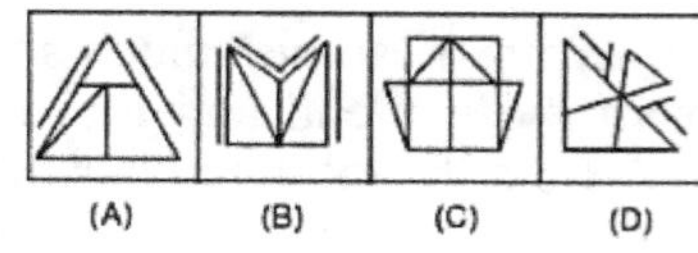

(A) A   (B) B
(C) C   (D) D

OLYMPIAD WORKBOOK (IMO) CLASS– 3

40. Find out the alternative figure which contains figure (X) as its part.

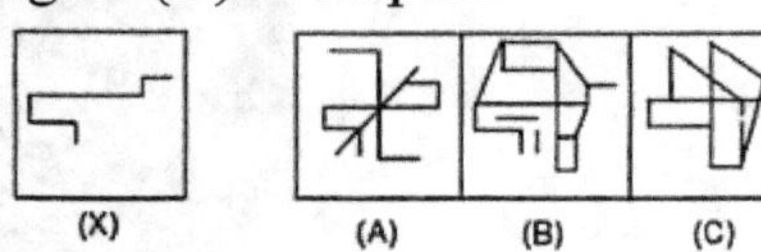

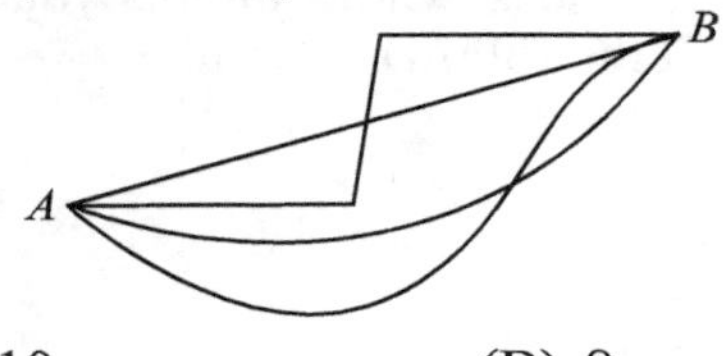

(A) A   (B) B
(C) C   (D) D

41. How many different ways can you reach from point A to point B?

(A) 10   (B) 8
(C) 9   (D) 11

42. There are 8 students in the class room. Each students shook hands once with each other. How many handshakes took place?

(A) 30
(B) 36
(C) 25
(D) 28

43. Five friends met and they greeted each other by saying 'What's up'. How many times was the word 'what's up' said?

(A) 10   (B) 15
(C) 20   (D) 19

44. How many possible combinations of 1 pen and 1 eraser can be formed from the given pens and erasers?

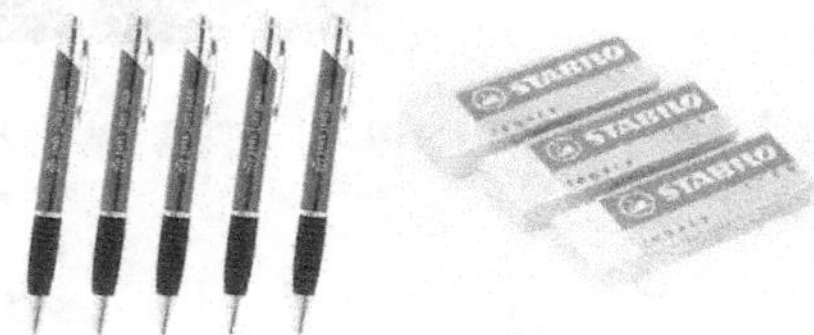

(A) 10   (B) 15
(C) 8   (D) 13

45. How many possible combinations of 1 bat and 1 ball can be formed from the given bats and balls?

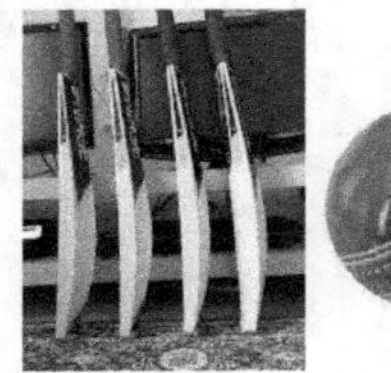 

(A) 10   (B) 7
(C) 32   (D) 12

1.	Ⓐ Ⓑ Ⓒ Ⓓ	10.	Ⓐ Ⓑ Ⓒ Ⓓ	19.	Ⓐ Ⓑ Ⓒ Ⓓ	28.	Ⓐ Ⓑ Ⓒ Ⓓ	37.	Ⓐ Ⓑ Ⓒ Ⓓ
2.	Ⓐ Ⓑ Ⓒ Ⓓ	11.	Ⓐ Ⓑ Ⓒ Ⓓ	20.	Ⓐ Ⓑ Ⓒ Ⓓ	29.	Ⓐ Ⓑ Ⓒ Ⓓ	38.	Ⓐ Ⓑ Ⓒ Ⓓ
3.	Ⓐ Ⓑ Ⓒ Ⓓ	12.	Ⓐ Ⓑ Ⓒ Ⓓ	21.	Ⓐ Ⓑ Ⓒ Ⓓ	30.	Ⓐ Ⓑ Ⓒ Ⓓ	39.	Ⓐ Ⓑ Ⓒ Ⓓ
4.	Ⓐ Ⓑ Ⓒ Ⓓ	13.	Ⓐ Ⓑ Ⓒ Ⓓ	22.	Ⓐ Ⓑ Ⓒ Ⓓ	31.	Ⓐ Ⓑ Ⓒ Ⓓ	40.	Ⓐ Ⓑ Ⓒ Ⓓ
5.	Ⓐ Ⓑ Ⓒ Ⓓ	14.	Ⓐ Ⓑ Ⓒ Ⓓ	23.	Ⓐ Ⓑ Ⓒ Ⓓ	32.	Ⓐ Ⓑ Ⓒ Ⓓ	41.	Ⓐ Ⓑ Ⓒ Ⓓ
6.	Ⓐ Ⓑ Ⓒ Ⓓ	15.	Ⓐ Ⓑ Ⓒ Ⓓ	24.	Ⓐ Ⓑ Ⓒ Ⓓ	33.	Ⓐ Ⓑ Ⓒ Ⓓ	42.	Ⓐ Ⓑ Ⓒ Ⓓ
7.	Ⓐ Ⓑ Ⓒ Ⓓ	16.	Ⓐ Ⓑ Ⓒ Ⓓ	25.	Ⓐ Ⓑ Ⓒ Ⓓ	34.	Ⓐ Ⓑ Ⓒ Ⓓ	43.	Ⓐ Ⓑ Ⓒ Ⓓ
8.	Ⓐ Ⓑ Ⓒ Ⓓ	17.	Ⓐ Ⓑ Ⓒ Ⓓ	26.	Ⓐ Ⓑ Ⓒ Ⓓ	35.	Ⓐ Ⓑ Ⓒ Ⓓ	44.	Ⓐ Ⓑ Ⓒ Ⓓ
9.	Ⓐ Ⓑ Ⓒ Ⓓ	18.	Ⓐ Ⓑ Ⓒ Ⓓ	27.	Ⓐ Ⓑ Ⓒ Ⓓ	36.	Ⓐ Ⓑ Ⓒ Ⓓ	45.	Ⓐ Ⓑ Ⓒ Ⓓ

MODEL TEST PAPER

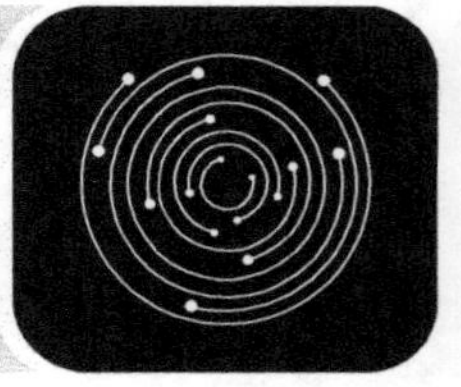

1. Which is the ninth object from the last?

   First   Last

   (A)   (B)

   (C)   (D)

2. In the given picture grid which word describes the position of 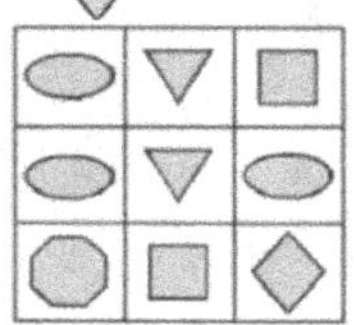?

   (A) Top centre   (B) Top left

   (C) Bottom right   (D) Centre left

3. If you look at this object from the top, what will you see?

   (A)   (B)

   (C)   (D)

4. Look at this pattern

    . Which is the missing part?

   (A) ☆◇△   (B) △△△

   (C) ☆△△   (D) ☆☆☆

5. What is the least whole number you can make using all the following number?

       3   5   1

   (A) 135

   (B) 315

   (C) 531

   (D) 351

6. The Tiger scored fewer points than the Dolphins but more points than Eagles. Which team has scored the most points?

   (A) The Dolphins

   (B) The Eagles

   (C) The Tigers

   (D) Both Tigers and Dolphins

7. Rohit has the given amount of money shown here. If the prices shown include Tax, which one of the following shirts can be buying with this money?

   (A) ₹ 100

   (B) ₹ 150

   (C) ₹ 180

   (D) ₹ 145

8. Look at the given Venn diagram. How many are hearts but not green?

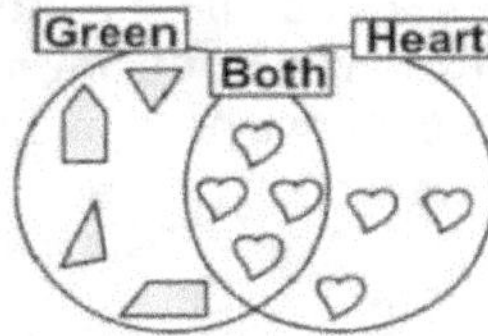

(A) 3 (B) 4
(C) 5 (D) 6

9. Rahul needs new toothpaste and some toothbrushes. He can choose from the given toothbrush colours and toothpaste flavours shown in the picture.

How many different combinations of 1 toothbrush colour and 1 toothpaste flavour are possible?

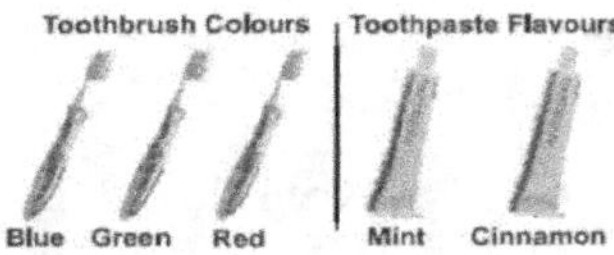

(A) 2 (B) 3
(C) 5 (D) 6

10. Third grade students made maps of Main Street. They used symbol for each office building, park and house.

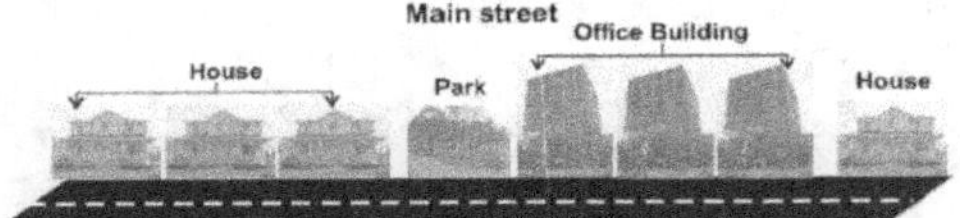

Which equation could be used to find out how many more office buildings are there than parks?

(A) 3 − 1 = 2 (B) 4 × 3 = 12
(C) 3 + 1 = 4 (D) 1 + 4 = 5

11. Which of the following figures is similar to the given figure?

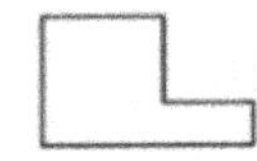

(A) (B)

(C) (D)

12. Which number sentence matches the given picture?

(A) 3 + 5 (B) 15 + 3
(C) 5 X 3 (D) 15 × 3

13. Look at Gaurav's timeline. What happens after Gaurav cleans the cabin and before he plays sand volleyball?

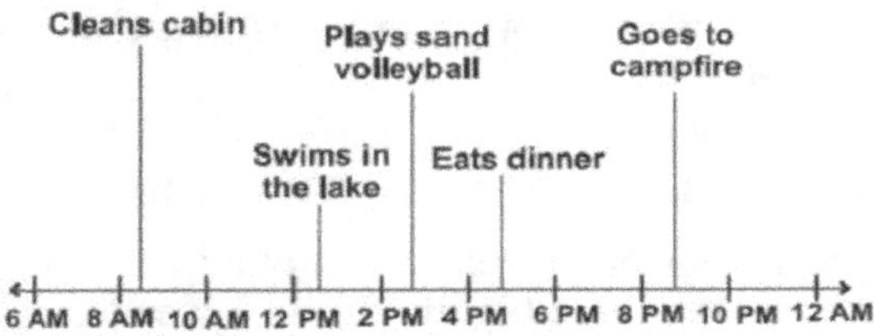

(A) Gaurav goes to the campfire.
(B) Gaurav eats Dinner.
(C) Gaurav swims in the lake.
(D) None of these.

14. Parul put 70 plastic cups in the first stack, 80 plastic cups in the second stack, and 90 plastic cups in the third stack. If this pattern continues, how many plastic cups will Parul put in the fourth stack?

(A) 100 (B) 108
(C) 106 (D) 107

15. How has this figure been transformed?

It has been _______
(A) Reflected (B) Rotated
(C) Translated (D) None of these

16. Which instrument you would use to find out how long will the train to arrive at the station?

(A) 

(B)

(C) 

(D)

17. Yesterday was Wednesday. What day is tomorrow?
(A) Thursday
(B) Friday
(C) Saturday
(D) Sunday.

18. Look at the given pattern.

How would you show this pattern using letters?
(A) AAB (B) AB
(C) ABC (D) ABB

19. Divya spent 1 week at a summer camp. What is the total number of days in 1 week?
(A) 7 (B) 2
(C) 5 (D) 8

20. Look at these numbers: 6,66,71,76 Which two numbers above have a sum of 137?
(A) 6 and 66
(B) 71 and 66
(C) 6 and 76
(D) 66 and 76

21. If a month ends on a Tuesday, on what day does the next month begin?
(A) Thursday (B) Monday
(C) Wednesday (D) Tuesday

22. Which of the given shapes represents a rectangle?

(A) (B)

(C) (D)

23. The distance around the middle of the Earth is 2757 kilometers. What is the place value of the digit 2 in the number 2757?
(A) 200 (B) 20
(C) 2 (D) 2000

24. Pulkit is having a birthday party. His mother told him that he could divide 30 stickers among the 4 friends he has invited. If pulkit gives each friend the same number of stickers, which picture shows how many stickers each friend will get?

(A) (B)

(C) (D)

25. The length of a shirt sleeve is best measured in _______
(A) Inches
(B) Millimeters
(C) Liters
(D) Grams

26. 1 2 3 4 5 6 7 8 9 10 11 12 13 14 15 16 17 18 19 20 21 22 23 24 25 26 27 28 29 30 31 32 33 34 35 36 37 38 39 40

Shally crosses out the numbers she says as she counts by 5(5, 10, ...) Next she will cross out all the even numbers on the chart above. Which one of the following number will she not cross out?
(A) 20 (B) 23
(C) 35 (D) 38

27. What is the missing number that makes the number sentence true ?
$$? + 19 + 7 = 33$$
(A) 6 (B) 7
(C) 58 (D) 59

28. What is another way to represent 6,204?
(A) $6 + 2 + 0 + 4$
(B) $60 + 20 + 10 + 4$
(C) $600 + 200 + 100 + 4$
(D) $6000 + 200 + 4$

29. Which letter can be folded in half, so that its side coincides?
(A) W (B) N
(C) L (D) S

30. Which is the closest distance from point M to point N on the number line?

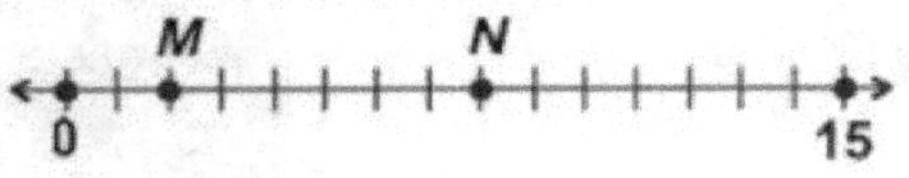

(A) 5 units   (B) 8 units
(C) 7 units   (D) 6 units

31. The clock shows the time 12:45. What time will it show after 45 min?

(A) 1:30   (B) 2:15
(C) 1:45 (D)   12:00

32. I am greater than 250 but less than 280. When you add my first and third digits you will get 9. Which number am I?
(A) 257   (B) 254
(C) 279   (D) 269

33. Rohan and Arjun played a Basketball game. They scored a total of 10 baskets. If Rohan scored 7 Baskets, then how many Baskets did Arjun score?
(A) 3
(B) 5
(C) 7
(D) 9

34. Romesh has 19 eggs. He has 2 empty egg cartons that can hold 12 eggs in each carton. How many more egg does Romesh need to fill the 2 egg cartons?
(A) 7
(B) 24
(C) 33
(D) 5

35. A snail can crawl 30 inches in 1 minute, if the snail crawls at this speed in one direction for 6 minutes, how far in inches, will it travel?
(A) 240 inches
(B) 180 inches
(C) 36 inches
(D) 5 inches

Darken Your Choice with HB Pencil

1.	Ⓐ Ⓑ Ⓒ Ⓓ	8.	Ⓐ Ⓑ Ⓒ Ⓓ	15.	Ⓐ Ⓑ Ⓒ Ⓓ	22.	Ⓐ Ⓑ Ⓒ Ⓓ	29.	Ⓐ Ⓑ Ⓒ Ⓓ
2.	Ⓐ Ⓑ Ⓒ Ⓓ	9.	Ⓐ Ⓑ Ⓒ Ⓓ	16.	Ⓐ Ⓑ Ⓒ Ⓓ	23.	Ⓐ Ⓑ Ⓒ Ⓓ	30.	Ⓐ Ⓑ Ⓒ Ⓓ
3.	Ⓐ Ⓑ Ⓒ Ⓓ	10.	Ⓐ Ⓑ Ⓒ Ⓓ	17.	Ⓐ Ⓑ Ⓒ Ⓓ	24.	Ⓐ Ⓑ Ⓒ Ⓓ	31.	Ⓐ Ⓑ Ⓒ Ⓓ
4.	Ⓐ Ⓑ Ⓒ Ⓓ	11.	Ⓐ Ⓑ Ⓒ Ⓓ	18.	Ⓐ Ⓑ Ⓒ Ⓓ	25.	Ⓐ Ⓑ Ⓒ Ⓓ	32.	Ⓐ Ⓑ Ⓒ Ⓓ
5.	Ⓐ Ⓑ Ⓒ Ⓓ	12.	Ⓐ Ⓑ Ⓒ Ⓓ	19.	Ⓐ Ⓑ Ⓒ Ⓓ	26.	Ⓐ Ⓑ Ⓒ Ⓓ	33.	Ⓐ Ⓑ Ⓒ Ⓓ
6.	Ⓐ Ⓑ Ⓒ Ⓓ	13.	Ⓐ Ⓑ Ⓒ Ⓓ	20.	Ⓐ Ⓑ Ⓒ Ⓓ	27.	Ⓐ Ⓑ Ⓒ Ⓓ	34.	Ⓐ Ⓑ Ⓒ Ⓓ
7.	Ⓐ Ⓑ Ⓒ Ⓓ	14.	Ⓐ Ⓑ Ⓒ Ⓓ	21.	Ⓐ Ⓑ Ⓒ Ⓓ	28.	Ⓐ Ⓑ Ⓒ Ⓓ	35.	Ⓐ Ⓑ Ⓒ Ⓓ

HINTS AND SOLUTIONS

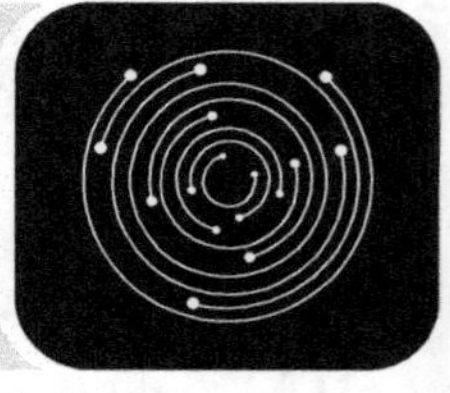

1. NUMBER SYSTEM

Answer Key

1. (B)	2. (C)	3. (A)	4. (B)	5. (A)	6. (A)	7. (A)	8. (B)	9. (B)	10. (B)
11. (A)	12. (B)	13. (C)	14. (B)	15. (B)	16. (D)	17. (B)	18. (A)	19. (C)	20. (A)

1. (B)

$\because$ 550 is divisible by 2. Hence 550 is an even number.

2. (C)

Here

(1) $7000 + 400 + 20 + 6 = 7426$
(2) $7000 + 400 + 00 + 6 = 7406$
(3) $700 + 60 + 6 = 766$
(4) $7000 + 000 + 60 + 7 = 7067$

3. (A)

We know that the largest 3 digit number is 999.

4. (B)

5 is an odd number.

5. (A)

$\because$ 102 is an even number and $\dfrac{102}{3} = 34$

6. (A)

Required sum $= 1 + 2 + 3 + 4 + 5 + 6 + 7 + 8 + 9 + 10 + 11 + 12 = 78$

7. (A)

Face value of 4 in 38, 455 $= 4$

8. (B)

We have $12554 = 12000 + 500 + 50 + 4$

9. (B)

Here 627 is the greatest three digit number.

10. (B)

Here 111 is the smallest three digit number.

11. (A)

Here $371 > 231$.

Solution $21 - 236$.

Given age of the boy $= 2$ years

Age of girl $= 2 + 3 = 5$ years

Father's age $= 7 \times 5 = 35$ years

Mother's age $= 35 - 3 = 32$ years

Grandfather's age $= 30 \times 2 = 60$ years

12. (B)

Odd numbers are 17, 9, 45, 19

$\because$ Required ascending order is
$$9, 17, 19, 45$$

13. (C)

Even numbers are $= 4, 22, 12, 34$

$\because$ Required in descending order is
$$34, 22, 12, 4$$

16. (D)

961 – Nine hundred sixty-one

HOTS (ACHIEVERS SECTION)

21. (D)	22. (C)	23. (B)	24. (D)	25. (D)

21. (D)

½ of 160 = ½ × 160 = 80

Half of 180 = 180 ÷ 2 = 90

12 × 13 = 156

2 times of (5× 5) = 25 × 2 = 50

Hence, option (d) has smallest value.

24. (D)

Option A = 1345

Option B = 5231

Option C = 1353

Option D = 1215

Hence, option (d) is value less than 1345

2. COMPUTATION OPERATIONS

Answer Key

1. (D)	2. (A)	3. (D)	4. (C)	5. (A)	6. (D)	7. (B)	8. (A)	9. (B)	10. (A)
11. (B)	12. (B)	13. (A)	14. (A)	15. (C)	16. (C)	17. (D)	18. (A)	19. (C)	20. (B)

1. (D)

Here 125 + 1508 = 1633

∴ ? = 2407 − 1633 = 774

2. (A)

We see

4 + 5 = 9

40 + 50 = 90

400 + 500 = 900

40000 + 50000 = 90000

4. (C)

Add 13

5. (A)

5746 + 2222 = 7968 and

3984 + 3984 = 7978   (False)

(B) 777 + 7777 = 8554   (True)

(C) 89 + 6789 = 6878   (False)

(D) 3000 + 175 = 3175 and

2981 + 179 = 3160   (False)

7. (B)

The given series is

6 − 5, 60 − 50, 600 − 500, 6000 − 5000

∴ 1, 10, 100, 1000

HOTS (ACHIEVERS SECTION)

21. (C)	22. (A)	23. (B)	24. (B)	25. (D)

3. FRACTIONS

Answer Key

1. (C)	2. (D)	3. (A)	4. (C)	5. (C)	6. (A)	7. (B)	8. (B)	9. (C)	10. (C)
11. (D)	12. (A)	13. (C)	14. (B)	15. (A)	16. (D)	17. (D)	18. (B)	19. (A)	20. (C)

1. (C)

Given $\dfrac{N}{6}$ and $\dfrac{2}{3}$ are equivalent

∴ $\dfrac{N}{6} = \dfrac{2}{3}$ is $N = 6 \times \dfrac{2}{3} = 4$

3. (A)

Here LCM of 3,6,2 and 7 is 42

∴ $\dfrac{1}{3}, \dfrac{1}{6}, \dfrac{1}{2}, \dfrac{1}{7} = \dfrac{14}{42}, \dfrac{7}{42}, \dfrac{21}{42}, \dfrac{6}{42}$

∴ Correct order is $\dfrac{21}{42}, \dfrac{14}{42}, \dfrac{7}{42}, \dfrac{6}{42}$

$= \dfrac{1}{2}, \dfrac{1}{3}, \dfrac{1}{6}$ and $\dfrac{1}{7}$

HINTS AND SOLUTIONS

5. **(C)**

Here $\dfrac{1}{4} : \dfrac{2}{8} :: \dfrac{1}{3} : ?$

$\therefore \ \dfrac{1}{4} = \dfrac{2}{2} \times \dfrac{1}{4} = \dfrac{2}{8}$ then $? = \dfrac{2 \times 1}{2 \times 3} = \dfrac{2}{6}$

6. **(A)**

$\therefore \ \dfrac{3}{4} = \dfrac{1}{3/4} = \dfrac{4}{3}$ then $? = \dfrac{1}{2/5} = \dfrac{5}{2}$

7. **(B)**

$\dfrac{1}{2} : \dfrac{1}{4} :: \dfrac{1}{5} : ? \Rightarrow ? = \dfrac{1}{2 \times 5} = \dfrac{1}{10}$

8. **(B)**

Required hours in a day $= \dfrac{24}{2} = 12$ hours

16. **(D)**

Required pizza $= 2 - \dfrac{2}{4} + \dfrac{3}{4} = 2 - \dfrac{5}{4}$

$= \dfrac{8-5}{4} = \dfrac{3}{4}$ of a pizza

HOTS (ACHIEVERS SECTION)				
21. (C)	22. (B)	23. (D)	24. (B)	25. (B)

4. MONEY

Answer Key

1. (D)	2. (B)	3. (B)	4. (D)	5. (D)	6. (C)	7. (C)	8. (A)	9. (A)	10. (A)
11. (D)	12. (B)	13. (D)	14. (C)	15. (B)	16. (C)	17. (B)	18. (B)	19. (D)	20. (B)

1. **(D)**

Total Money $= ₹2.75 + 2 \times 7.50$

$= 2.75 + 15.00 = ₹17.75$

2. **(B)**

Cost of 4 chocolates

$= 4 \times$ cost of 1 chocolate

$= 4 \times 7.50 = ₹30$

and cost of 2 pencils $= 2 \times 5.50$

Hence, false.

3. **(B)**

Required No. of clocks

$= \dfrac{500}{170} = 2 \ (₹160)$

5. **(D)**

Total money

$= ₹(5 + 10 + 20 + 50 + 500 + 0.50 + 0.25)$

$= ₹585.75$

7. **(C)**

The correct order is ₹0.75, ₹1.50, ₹1.75, ₹2.25, ₹2.50, ₹2.75

16. **(C)**

There are 30 days in September.

Required amount $= 5 \times 30 = ₹150$

18. **(B)**

Required amount

$= ₹(3 \times 100 + 20 \times 2 + 4 \times 2)$

$= -₹326$

$= ₹[(300 + 40 + 8) - 326] = ₹22$

19. **(D)**

Cost of 1 chocolate $= \dfrac{88.50}{6} = 14.75$

$= ₹14$ and 75 paise

21. (B)	22. (D)	23. (B)	24. (A)	25. (A)

5. LENGTH, WEIGHT, CAPACITY & TIME

Answer Key

1. (B)	2. (C)	3. (C)	4. (B)	5. (A)	6. (A)	7. (B)	8. (C)	9. (B)	10. (C)
11. (D)	12. (A)	13. (D)	14. (C)	15. (C)	16. (A)	17. (C)	18. (A)	19. (A)	20. (D)

1. **(B)**
Shorts requires minimum length of cloth

2. **(C)**
Statement B is incorrect

5. **(A)**
We know standard unit of length is meter.

6. **(A)**
The correct order is ACDB.

9. **(B)**
Tripti weighted her pumpkin on the scale and found it was 7 kg. Hence pumpkin's cost is ₹40.

10. **(C)**
Pumpkin's cost = 12000 gm = 12 kg
∴   Rate is ₹60.

11. **(D)**
∵ 2540 mL = 2000 mL + 540 mL
= 2 L + 540 mL
= 2 L, 540 mL
∴ 1 L 5 mL = (1000 + 5) mL = 1005 mL

13. **(D)**

Capacity of bucket = $\dfrac{45}{5} = 9$ L

21. (A)	22. (D)	23. (C)	24. (D)	25. (B)

6. GEOMETRY

Answer Key

1. (A)	2. (D)	3. (C)	4. (A)	5. (B)	6. (C)	7. (D)	8. (B)	9. (C)	10. (D)
11. (C)	12. (A)	13. (A)	14. (A)	15. (B)	16. (B)	17. (C)	18. (B)	19. (C)	20. (D)

21. (C)	22. (A)	23. (A)	24. (A)	25. (B)

Answer Key

1. (C)	2. (B)	3. (D)	4. (A)	5. (B)	6. (A)	7. (A)	8. (C)	9. (B)	10. (A)
11. (C)	12. (B)	13. (C)	14. (B)	15. (D)	16. (B)	17. (A)	18. (B)	19. (D)	20. (A)

1. **(C)**
   Rohan reads 20 books
   Manu reads 15 books
   so, the answer is 20 − 15
   $$= 5 \text{ books.}$$

7. **(A)**
   $\because$ 0 = 2 students
   $\Rightarrow$ 00 = 4 students

20. **(A)**
   Red coloured pen is least liked by children.

HOTS (ACHIEVERS SECTION)

21. (A)	22. (A)	23. (B)	24. (A)	

8. LOGICAL REASONING

Answer Key

1. (C)	2. (D)	3. (B)	4. (C)	5. (B)	6. (B)	7. (C)	8. (D)	9. (A)	10. (C)
11. (A)	12. (C)	13. (D)	14. (B)	15. (A)	16. (A)	17. (D)	18. (A)	19. (C)	20. (C)
21. (D)	22. (B)	23. (A)	24. (D)	25. (C)	26. (B)	27. (C)	28. (A)	29. (D)	30. (B)
31. (C)	32. (C)	33. (D)	34. (B)	35. (C)	36. (D)	37. (A)	38. (D)	39. (C)	40. (C)
41. (B)	42. (D)	43. (A)	44. (B)	45. (D)					

6. **(B)**
   There is a gap of one alphabet between A and C. So, the answer is Z because there is gap of one alphabet between X and Z.

12. **(C)**
   The capital of India is Delhi but Delhi is calld Lucknow.

14. **(B)**
   Bee gives honey to us but Bee is called Tiger.

16. **(A)**
   D is not given in REINVEST.

17. **(D)**
   A occurs twice in APPEARING.

20. **(C)**
   Conceit comes first in the given word.

21. **(D)**
   Total keys = 24
   Also, $3 \times \boxed{8} = 24$
   Thus 8 bunches of 3 keys can be formed.

22. (B)

Total bats = 24

Also $4 \times \boxed{6} = 24$

Thus, 6 groups of 4 bats can be formed.

26. (B)

Ram Govind Shyam Mukesh

left

So, Govind is sitting at 2nd position from left end.

30. (B)

Ram's position from left end = 2nd

So, number of students in left of Ram = 1

Position of Ram from right end = 4th

So, number of students in his right = 3

Hence, total students = 1 + 3 + (Ram) = 5

MODEL TEST PAPER

Answer Key

1. (C)	2. (C)	3. (A)	4. (A)	5. (A)	6. (A)	7. (A)	8. (A)	9. (D)	10. (A)
11. (B)	12. (C)	13. (C)	14. (A)	15. (A)	16. (B)	17. (B)	18. (A)	19. (A)	20. (B)
21. (C)	22. (A)	23. (D)	24. (C)	25. (A)	26. (B)	27. (B)	28. (D)	29. (A)	30. (D)
31. (A)	32. (A)	33. (A)	34. (D)	35. (B)					

SAMPLE OMR ANSWER SHEET

1. STUDENT NAME (IN ENGLISH CAPITAL LETTERS ONLY)

Students must write and darken the respective circles completely using HB Pencil only. Othewise their Answer Sheets will not be evaluated.

PERSONAL DETAILS

2. SCHOOL CODE

3. CLASS

4. SECTION

5. ROLL NO.

6. QUESTION PAPER SET

A ○
B ○
C ○
D ○

7. MOBILE NUMBER

8. GENDER

MALE ○
FEMALE ○

9. STREAM
(Only for Class XI and XII Students)

MATHEMATICS ○
BIOLOGY ○
OTHERS ○

MARK YOUR ANSWERS

1.	A	B	C	D	26.	A	B	C	D
2.	A	B	C	D	27.	A	B	C	D
3.	A	B	C	D	28.	A	B	C	D
4.	A	B	C	D	29.	A	B	C	D
5.	A	B	C	D	30.	A	B	C	D
6.	A	B	C	D	31.	A	B	C	D
7.	A	B	C	D	32.	A	B	C	D
8.	A	B	C	D	33.	A	B	C	D
9.	A	B	C	D	34.	A	B	C	D
10.	A	B	C	D	35.	A	B	C	D
11.	A	B	C	D	36.	A	B	C	D
12.	A	B	C	D	37.	A	B	C	D
13.	A	B	C	D	38.	A	B	C	D
14.	A	B	C	D	39.	A	B	C	D
15.	A	B	C	D	40.	A	B	C	D
16.	A	B	C	D	41.	A	B	C	D
17.	A	B	C	D	42.	A	B	C	D
18.	A	B	C	D	43.	A	B	C	D
19.	A	B	C	D	44.	A	B	C	D
20.	A	B	C	D	45.	A	B	C	D
21.	A	B	C	D	46.	A	B	C	D
22.	A	B	C	D	47.	A	B	C	D
23.	A	B	C	D	48.	A	B	C	D
24.	A	B	C	D	49.	A	B	C	D
25.	A	B	C	D	50.	A	B	C	D

Signature of the Student & Date of Examination

Signature of the Invigilator & Date of Examination

www.ingramcontent.com/pod-product-compliance
Lightning Source LLC
Chambersburg PA
CBHW081303130726

47998CB00010B/2913

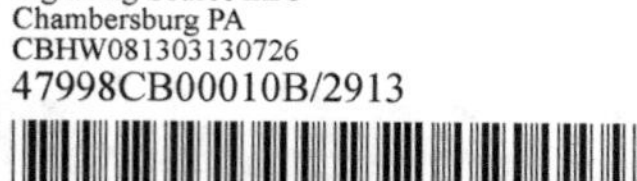